THE LATE
MRS EARLY

A Comedy

NORMAN ROBBINS

SAMUEL   FRENCH

LONDON
NEW YORK TORONTO SYDNEY HOLLYWOOD

MADE AND PRINTED IN GREAT BRITAIN BY
LATIMER TREND & COMPANY LTD PLYMOUTH
MADE IN ENGLAND

CHARACTERS

Terry Early
Susan Rickworth
Mabel Sutton
Sam Early
Alice Louise Early
Joe Gittings
Reuben Rickworth
Lucy Rickworth

The action of the play passes in the living-room of the Early's terraced council house, Catlow Street, Castleford, Yorkshire

ACT I

ACT II

Time – the present

AUTHOR'S NOTE

Although the characters and events contained in this play are fictitious, the town of Castleford does exist. It is a small mining district in West Yorkshire, and over twenty years of my life were spent there.

Hightown, Wilkinson's sweet shop, Catlow Street and the Commercial Hotel (which, incidentally, was hosted by my grandparents) were familiar names of my childhood, but town development has removed most of these links, and replaced them with parkland and factories.

As a small attempt to keep alive happy memories, I have used these names freely, and would like to dedicate this play to the one-time residents of that lost area and in particular to Muriel and Hilda Barnes of Ponteract, who have done more to encourage and sustain the Arts in that district than anyone else I know. My sincere thanks.

However, I have no objection to Directors of this work changing street names and districts to suit their own areas, if so required, though of course, I would prefer the originals.

NORMAN ROBBINS
1975

PS. We even had a reputed haunted house.

ACT I

SCENE 1

The living-room of the Early's terraced council house, Catlow Street, Castleford, Yorkshire. Saturday morning

The house is one of a long row of terrace houses erected about a century ago by the local council. The room is oblong, and the only window in it is set in the centre of the wall L. This looks out on to a view of the street, and a railway shunting and stockyard beyond. Two doors in the back wall, L and R, are the only means of entrance and exit. These lead off into a long narrow passage, which in turn leads to the kitchen and rest of the house. A glimpse of the stairs may be seen when the door L is open. The fireplace, a fairly modern one and therefore slightly out of place, is in the wall R, facing the window. Fire irons stand in a compendium. The room is clean and neat, but somewhat cheerless. The paper is of the faded roses type, and wall brackets and a few almost period pictures are all that break the monotony. In front of the window is a square, dark oak table. Three chairs to match are placed one above the table facing the audience, one facing the window, and one below the table facing its partner. A red chenille cloth covers the table top and a cheap vase containing a bunch of badly made imitation flowers is set in the centre of it. Net curtains, slightly yellowed, hang at the window, and thick curtains hang at each side for night-time use. Between the two doors is a heavy oak sideboard and on it stands a framed photo of Alice and Sam on their wedding day, and an old-fashioned clock. A small hideous vase, most probably an unwanted gift from the seaside, stands opposite the photo. In the corner of the room R, is a small table. On this stands an old-fashioned radio set. On top of the fireplace is a collection of tiny brass objects, all sparkling bright. A mirror hangs above them. Below the fireplace, a bright red plastic pouffe stands. At an angle to the fireplace, the heavy sofa faces front. Large cushions which clash violently are on it, and an antimacassar is draped along its back. The floor is carpeted with good but hard wearing covering and scatter rugs. Light switches by both doors. An ugly lightshade hangs from the centre of the tiled ceiling

When the CURTAIN *rises the room is empty and the fire is lit. After a moment, the door L is pushed open, and Terry Early cautiously sticks his head into the room. Seeing no-one is about, he pushes the door wide open and jauntily steps into the room. He is about seventeen, dressed in figure-hugging jeans, bright sweater and plimsolls. After a further quick look around, he turns to the door again, sticks his head into the passage and calls*

Terry It's all right, Susan. You can come in.

Terry moves back to allow Susan Rickworth to enter. She is a very pretty girl of seventeen, dressed in a neat skirt and blouse, and carrying a small purse

Susan (*nervously*) Are you sure it's all right, Terry?

Terry (*flopping on to the sofa*) Course it is. I told you. There's nobody in at all. (*He pats the sofa beside him*) Come on. Sit down.

Susan (*doubtfully*) I don't know . . .

Terry What are you worried about? It's not me mother, is it?

Susan Well . . .

Terry Look, I told you. She's gone over to me Aunt Ethel's. She'll be out for hours.

Susan How about your dad, though?

Terry Ah . . . you don't have to bother yourself about me dad. (*He pats the sofa again*) Come on.

Susan perches beside him, looking uncomfortable

Relax, can't you? Look—we'll have to tell him about it sooner or later, won't we? So *he* can break the news to Mum.

Susan (*suddenly*) Couldn't we just elope, Terry, and get it over with?

Terry Elope? What do you want to elope for? We can get married here in Castleford as well as anywhere else, can't we?

Susan Yes, I know—but—well . . . It's just the thought of facing your mother. I don't mind your dad so much, but . . .

Terry (*taking her hand*) Look. It's not as if we've *got* to get married, is it? I mean that would *really* make her blow her top. The fact is—we *want* to get married, and that makes all the difference.

Susan looks doubtful

Anyway, I don't see why she *should* kick up a fuss about it. It's not you she's got a grudge against. She's never even met you.

Susan That's the whole point, Terry. I'm scared of what she's going to say when she finds out it's me you want to marry.

Terry (*laughing*) What can she say? She must know I'm going to get married some time, so what's wrong with getting engaged now?

Susan (*exasperated*) Oh don't act so thick, Terry. You know what the positión's like with your mum and dad and mine. They haven't spoken to each other for nineteen years, so how do you think they're going to react to a thing like this?

Terry (*darkly*) Probably with wholesale murder. It'll be like Romeo and Juliet all over again. Corpses littering the stage. (*With great drama*) The rest is silence. (*He falls back on the sofa, eyes closed as if in death*)

Susan That's Hamlet.

Terry (*opening his eyes*) Oh. (*He sits up again*)

Susan It's going to be bad enough facing my mum and dad—but *yours* . . .

Terry There won't be any problem with me dad. He'll be only too pleased for us—but Mum . . . (*He shakes his head slightly*)

Susan Why should your dad be pleased for us?

Terry Why shouldn't he be? I mean—the row's got nothing to do with him, has it? It's between my mum and yours.

Susan I don't think so. I thought it was your dad and mum and my dad.

Terry My dad? Don't be daft. My dad's never fallen out with anybody in his life. He's far too interested in his flipping rose growing to waste time rowing with folks. No. It's Mum that wears the trousers in this house. If there's any rowing to be done, it'll be *her* that's doing it.

Susan I wonder what it was all about. You know. Why they fell out.

Terry I don't know. The only thing I *do* know is whenever somebody mentions your dad's name, Mum goes spare. Anyway, never mind about all that. That's their problem. We've got much more important things to be getting on with.

Susan Such as?

Terry Well, we've got the house to ourselves, for a start, haven't we? So why don't we take advantage of it, and get down to a bit of serious pre-engagement snogging? I've been waiting for this moment all week. (*He pulls her close*)

Susan (*drawing back*) Just a minute.

Terry What?

Susan I've just thought on. How can your dad grow roses? You haven't got a garden.

Terry (*groaning*) Oh, blimey. He shares an allotment with old Mr Gittings down the street.

Susan Doesn't he ever bring any home? For the house?

Terry No. Mum doesn't like 'em.

Susan Doesn't she like roses?

Terry She doesn't like *any* flowers. In the house, that is. Not live ones, anyway. That's why she has them cheap plastic things over there. (*He points*) I think she gets 'em with the soap powder or something. Now stop playing hard to get and come here. (*He once more pulls her to him and they kiss*)

Susan (*breaking away*) I wonder why?

Terry Why what?

Susan Why she doesn't like fresh flowers?

Terry (*sighing*) Because she says they remind her of funerals.

Susan Why's that?

Terry (*tired*) How should I know. Ask her when you see her. I suppose it's because she takes a big bunch up to me grandma's grave once a month. Now come on. (*He pulls her back to him*) If we don't look sharp there'll be somebody coming home..

Susan (*smiling*) Sorry.

They kiss again

As they are locked together, the door R *opens and Mabel Sutton peers in. She is a thin-lipped woman of forty-five, wearing a cheap print dress underneath a grubby housecoat. Her hair, which is in rollers, peeps out from beneath a turban. A cigarette droops from her lips. She steps into the room and sees the two figures on the sofa. In order to get a better view, she moves to the top end of the sofa. After a few moments, she coughs*

Mabel Ahem.

Terry and Susan spring apart. Terry scrambles to his feet

Terry (*embarrassed*) Oh! Hello, Mrs Sutton. Er—can I help you?
Mabel (*with a thin smile*) Looks to me as if you're too busy helping yourself.

Terry gives a sickly grin

I take it your mother's not home?
Terry No.
Mabel (*nodding*) I thought not. (*She glances at Susan*)
Terry (*intercepting the glance*) Oh—er—Mrs Sutton. This is Susan. Susan Rickworth. My—er—my fiancée.
Susan (*nervously*) Hello.
Mabel (*eyeing her thoughtfully*) Rickworth, eh? (*To Susan*) You—er—you wouldn't be any relative of them Rickworths from up Hightown, would you? The ones what keep that tripe shop?
Terry That's right, Mrs Sutton. Susan's their daughter.
Mabel (*her eyes lighting up*) Reuben and Lucy Rickworth? Well, well, well. Now *that's* what I call a *real* turn up for the books, and *no* mistake.
Susan Do you know my parents, then?
Mabel (*with a mirthless smile*) Well—let's just say—I know *of* them. Come to think of it—there's not many folks around here as *doesn't* know of them. (*To Terry*) Is there, young Terry?
Terry Well—maybe there isn't, Mrs Sutton. But that's got nothing to do with Susan.
Mabel I don't know if your mother would agree with *that* statement, but I wouldn't mind placing a little bet on it. You—er—you *have* told her, I take it?
Terry No. Not yet. But I'm going to tell her today. The minute she gets back.
Mabel I can't wait.
Terry She can't possibly have anything against Susan.
Mabel "Sins of the fathers", and all that.
Susan (*blankly*) Sorry? I don't understand.
Mabel No—I don't suppose you do, love. After all—you'd be the *last* one they'd think of telling, wouldn't you?
Susan Telling what?
Mabel (*shaking her head*) Least said, soonest mended, that's my motto. And in any case. What you don't know, can't really hurt you, can it?
Terry Are you trying to *say* something, Mrs Sutton?
Mabel (*surprised*) Say something? Me? Whatever gave you that idea, young Terry? It's nothing to do with me. Live and let live, is what I always say. Let them without sin throw the first stone.

Terry Sin? (*Firmly*) Now look here . . .

Mabel (*sharply*) There's no need to raise your voice, Terry Early. I'm not deaf yet.

Terry Just what are you getting at?

Mabel Getting at? I'm not getting at anything. But if you must know, I shall be very surprised to say the least, if Alice Early agrees to let her son marry a girl whose mother only just made it to the altar in time.

Susan (*rising*) Oh.

Terry (*grimly*) I think you'd better go, Mrs Sutton.

Mabel Oh, yes. You'll want to be alone, won't you? While you've got the chance. I'll pop back later though to see your mother. I shall be most interested to hear all the details. (*She turns to go*)

Susan It's not true, Terry. I was just a bit premature.

Mabel (*turning again*) Premature? Well, that's a new name for it I suppose, but I'll tell you this much for nothing. If you'd have been any more premature, you could have been one of the bridesmaids.

Mabel exits R

Susan Oh, Terry . . . It's not true.

Terry Of course it's not. But what if it was? What difference would it make? It wouldn't make me love you any the less.

Susan I know—but what if your mother . . .

Terry Oh, blow me mother. It's me you're going to marry . . . not her. Now come on. Give us another kiss and stop blubbering.

Susan (*stung*) I'm not blubbering.

Terry Well then.

Terry and Susan go into a standing embrace

The door L *opens and Sam Early enters. He is about forty years old, dressed in an old suit and cardigan, and carries a gardening magazine which he reads avidly. He sits on the sofa without noticing Terry and Susan*

Terry and Susan begin to subside onto the sofa, still locked in their embrace. As they finally drop on top of Sam, all three react, then struggle to stand

Terry (*gulping*) Dad!

Sam (*glancing at Susan*) Sorry, lad. Didn't mean to interrupt. (*He moves towards the door* L *again*)

Terry (*quickly*) No—don't go, Dad. We've got something to tell you.

Sam (*turning*) Oh?

Terry (*taking Susan's hand*) Dad—this is Susan. Susan—me dad.

Sam How do. (*He nods*)

Susan (*timidly*) Hello.

Terry She—er—she comes from up Hightown.

Sam Oh, aye.

Terry Yes. In fact—you—er—you know her parents.

Sam Do I?

Terry Mr and Mrs Rickworth.

Sam Oh, yes . . . (*He realizes*) Rickworth? Not tripe shop Rickworths? (*He looks in horror at them both*)

Terry That's right, Dad. And we're going to get married.

Sam (*sinking into a chair*) Married?

Terry (*brightly*) Aren't you going to congratulate us?

Sam (*trembling*) Never mind about congratulating you. If your mother comes in and sees her here, I'll be *cremating* you. Oh, Terry, lad. Whatever were you thinking of bringing the lass round here? (*Jumping up*) Quick. Get her out.

Terry But, Dad. We're engaged.

Sam (*almost in tears*) Engaged, he says. Lad—she'll murder you.

Terry Well, why shouldn't I get engaged? I'm nearly eighteen, aren't I? Another few months and I'll be able to do what I want, anyway.

Sam Yes—if you manage to *live* that long. Oh, Terry . . .

Terry But, Dad . . .

Sam Why, lad? Why? Of all the lasses there are in this district, why did you have to go and choose this one? (*To Susan*) Nothing against you, love, but . . .

Terry (*angrily*) What's wrong with getting engaged to Susan?

Sam Nothing, lad, as far as I'm concerned. She looks a bonny lass and her folks are the most respectable in Castleford—but your mother . . .

Terry What about her?

Sam You *know* what about her, lad. If anybody so much as mentions the name Rickworth when she's in earshot, the balloon goes up.

Terry But why? What's wrong with them? What have they done?

Sam (*resigned*) Well, I don't suppose it'll do any harm to tell you, but whatever you do, don't let on to your mother I've opened my mouth about it. I've got enough bother on with her as it is. Sit down. The both of you.

Terry and Susan sit on the sofa

It's like this. Your dad, Susan, was engaged to my wife before he got married to your mother. I don't know the ins and outs of it all, but it seems that six weeks before they were due to get wed, he jilted her, and ran off with your mother. She's never forgiven him for that, so can you imagine what she's going to say when our Terry tells her he wants to marry you?

Terry But that's got nothing to do with Susan, Dad. She can't blame her for that. And anyway, that was nineteen years ago.

Sam What's nineteen years to a woman like your mother? She's got the mind of an elephant when it comes to an insult. (*He sighs*) If it were up to me, son, I'd tell you to get on with it. But it isn't. You know what she's going to say.

Terry Couldn't you talk to her?

Sam Me? Nay, lad. The last time she listened to me was nineteen years ago—and that were only to hear if I said "I do" without hesitating.

Susan So—it's no use then?

Sam (*shaking his head*) I'm sorry, love.

Terry Well you could at least *try* to make her see reason, Dad. We're not going to call the whole thing off because of what she *might* say.

Sam There's no *might* about it, lad. And since when has your mother been able to see any reason but her own? No—best thing you can do is just stay good friends—and don't let your mother find out about it.

Susan Good friends?

Terry But we're in love, Dad—and in any case—she's going to find out about it soon enough. Old Mother Sutton from next door's been in and seen us together.

Sam (*groaning*) That's all we need. She'll have grabbed her megaphone and be spreading the news all over town.

Terry So what? We don't care who knows about us because we're going to get married no matter what my mother has to say, so the sooner she hears about it the better.

Alice (*off*) *Terry!*

They all gaze at one another in horror

Sam She's heard. (*He dashes for the door* R)

The door L *flies open violently, and Alice Louise Early barges in. She is a large, battle-axe of a woman, aged about forty-two or three. She wears a thick sensible coat over a print dress, and a hat is crushed down on her head. She carries a wicker basket which contains groceries. Her face is grim*

Alice (*to Sam*) Stay where you are.

Sam stops dead in his tracks

Terry (*weakly*) Hello, Mum.

Alice (*slamming her basket down on the table*) So . . .

Sam Just a minute, Alice . . .

Alice (*snapping*) Quiet, you. I'm talking to the organ grinder, not the monkey. (*To Terry*) Well?

Terry Now calm down, Mum . . .

Alice (*loudly*) I am calm. I just want to know what you mean by telling Mabel Sutton that this—(*she indicates Susan*)—happened to be your fiancée?

Terry That's right, Mum. We're going to be married.

Alice How far gone is she?

Sam Here . . .

Alice Quiet! (*To Terry*) Well, come on. When's it due?

Terry When's what due?

Alice The baby.

Susan (*indignant*) I'm not pregnant.

Alice Well, that's all right, then, isn't it? Take your hook.

Terry Mum . . .

Alice I thought you had more sense, Terry Early. Letting an old trick like
that pull the wool over your eyes.

Terry There's no trick about it, Mum. Susan and me are in love.

Alice (*snorting*) Love. Ha. What does a kid like you know about love?
You're only just out of your nappies. (*To Susan*) I thought I told you
to go?

Terry If she goes, Mum, then I'm going as well. (*He takes her arm and
moves her to the door*)

Alice (*pulling him back*) Not so fast. You're not leaving this house until
I know that whatever it is between you two is over and done with.

Terry Well in that case you'd better get used to the idea of having Susan
around, Mother, because we're going to get married no matter what you
have to say about it.

Alice Oh, you are, are you? Well let me tell you this, Terry Early. Unless
you get that girl out of here in two minutes flat, I'm going down to
Castleford Police station to get you made into a Ward of Court. That'll
stop your little gallop.

Terry Ah, come off it, Mother. They don't go in for all that old-fashioned
stuff these days. They'd laugh in your face.

Alice Would they? Well just you go ahead, and we'll find out, won't we?

Terry And in any case—what good's that going to do? All it means is
that we'll have to get the Court's permission to marry, and that'll be
easy enough.

Alice Will it? (*She shakes her head*) It's not as simple as that, our Terry.
You'll have to prove you're fit to marry and can support a wife and
home; and I very much doubt if you can convince 'em of that—not on
an income of ten pounds forty-five a week.

Terry We'll manage.

Alice It's not a question of being able to manage. There's also the small
matter of one hundred and fifty pounds you owe me for that motorbike
of yours.

Sam Nay, Alice. Be right. We bought him that bike for his birthday.

Alice There's nobody asking you. (*To Terry*) Well?

Terry (*looking worried*) Like me dad said—you got me that bike for me
birthday. It was a present.

Alice Maybe it was—but he'll keep his mouth shut about it, won't you,
Sam? (*Warningly*) That is, if you know what's good for you. (*To Terry*)
Well, our Terry? What's it going to be? Are you going to see reason and
do as I tell you, or would you rather be a Ward of Court? It's entirely
up to you.

Terry looks at Susan in appeal, then back to Alice

Well, come on. Let's hear it.

Terry I—I don't know.

Susan (*softly*) I think I'd better go, Terry.

Terry Susan . . .

Susan It's no use. (*She turns*)

Terry Wait. We don't have to give up hope. There's only a few months to go before I can please myself *who* I get married to. We can hold on till then, can't we?

Susan It's not worth it, Terry. She'd find some other way of stopping you.

Alice You must be a gypsy. You can see yourself out, can't you? Terry— go put the kettle on.

Terry stands transfixed

Now!

Susan exits L, *closing the door behind her. Terry exits* R *slowly*

(*Calling*) And don't be all day about it. (*She takes off her coat and hat*) And now I'd like to have a quiet word with you, Sam Early.

Sam winces

Sit.

Sam sits on the sofa

How long has this been going on?

Sam How long has what been going on?

Alice Him—with her. (*She moves to him*)

Sam I've no idea.

Alice (*in a voice heavy with scorn*) Do you mean to tell me that your own son has been running around with that girl long enough for him to think he wants to marry her—and you didn't know about it?

Sam No. I'd never clapped eyes on her before.

Alice Well all I can say, Sam Early, is that you're either a liar or a fool— and I know which one of 'em *I* think it is.

Sam So do I. I were a fool ever to have married you, Alice. You've done nothing but make my life a misery since the day we got wed, and now you're starting on our Terry.

Alice Made *your* life a misery? And what about mine? What sort of a life do you think I've had? Slaving away over a hot stove every day for the last nineteen years. Washing, scrubbing, trying to make ends meet on what pittance you bring home each week. I've been a good wife to you, Sam Early, better than you'll ever know. Much, much better.

Sam I know you've worked wonders, Alice, but a chap wants to have a bit of peace once in a while. I can't even take a breath in me own house without asking your permission to do it. Hang it all. Our Terry's——

Alice (*interupting*) Too young to know his own mind, and as long as I've got any say in the running of this household, he'll do as I tell him . . . without argument. And that goes for you as well.

Sam Aye, you've got me well trained, haven't you?

Alice If I have, it's taken long enough. (*She turns away*) Anyway, there's only room for one boss in this family, and we all know who that is, don't we? (*Silence from Sam*) I said don't we?

Sam (*resignedly*) Yes, Alice.

Alice Right—and that's the way it's going to stay. (*She moves to the door* R *and opens it*) Terry? Terry?

Alice exits down the passage

(*Off*) Where are you? Terry?

She re-enters

He's gone out. (*She hurries to the window*) If he's gone chasing that Rickworth girl I'll wring his grubby little neck for him. (*She looks out*) He has. (*Rapping furiously on the glass*) Terry! Terry! (*She turns to Sam*) Just wait till he comes back.

Sam What makes you so sure he *will*?

Alice (*darkly*) He'd better.

Sam You'll push him that bit too much, one of these days. You can't tell youngsters what they can and what they can't do nowadays.

Alice Who says I can't? A good rattle round the earholes is what I'd give 'em all. They get far too much of their own way, these modern teenagers. Long-haired layabouts, that's all they are. Like him next door. Eustace Sutton. There's a perfect example of young British youth. Too idle to scratch himself. I blame the parents for it, but its not going to happen in this house. As long as our Terry stays here, he'll do as he's told.

There is a loud knocking on the back door off R

And if that's the insurance man, go tell him he's not getting anything this week. I'll pay him double next.

Sam (*tiredly*) Aye. (*He rises*)

Alice Well jump to it, then. By the time you get there he'll have started worrying in case he's got to pay out.

Sam exits

Alice moves to the table and moves the vase of flowers to the sideboard. She takes a cloth out of the drawer and covers the table. She then gets cups, saucers and plates from the sideboard cupboard, and begins to set them out

Sam enters R *followed by Joe Gittings. He is a typical retired working-class fellow, aged between sixty-five and seventy. He wears a pair of dirty, baggy trousers tucked into boots. A shapeless sweater over an old union shirt, and a flat cap. He is spectacled, and a pipe is stuck in his mouth*

Sam It's Joe.

Alice (*without turning*) And what's he want?

Joe (*brightly*) 'Lo, Alice.

Sam He's just popped round to see if I wanted to go down to the allotment with him.

Alice Oh. Well he can just pop back again. You'll be having your dinner in a few minutes.

Sam I wouldn't be long, Alice.

Alice (*turning to them*) I've told you. The answer's no. Good morning, Mr Gittings.

Sam But, Alice——

Alice (*loudly*) NO!

Joe Oh—well . . . (*He turns to leave*) I—er—I'll see you after then, p'raps?

Sam All right, Joe. Soon as dinner's over, eh?

Joe Aye.

Alice (*to Sam*) Aren't you forgetting something?

Sam Eh?

Alice I said, aren't you forgetting something?

Sam Like what?

Alice You happen to be coming out with *me* this afternoon—or had the occasion slipped your memory?

Sam looks blank

To the cemetery.

Sam Oh, Alice, can't you go on your own for once?

Alice No, I can't. She was a good woman was my mother, and she's going to get the respect paid to her that she's due. You haven't missed going up there with me for the last fifteen years, and you're not going to start missing now. Besides—I shall need your help to carry the flowers.

Joe How many are you thinking of taking?

Alice Nobody's talking to you, Joe Gittings—but while you *are* here, I might as well tell you that in future, you needn't bother to trundle your carcass around here every time you feel the urge for a free meal. I've got enough on trying to feed us lot on what he brings home each week, without trying to feed you as well.

Joe (*taken aback*) Well, by heck!

Alice And I'll have no cursing in my house, if you don't mind. There's far too much of it these days. Ever since your Renee died, you've come braying on our back door in the hopes of landing yourself a slap-up meal. I've put up with it till now because I'm a patient woman and I felt a bit sorry for you, but from now on it's going to stop. If you want to eat, you can either cough some money up, or you can stay at home and do it. (*To Sam*) I'm just going up to the chip shop, so you can finish laying the table. (*She puts her coat back on*) And don't put too much butter on the bread. It's not tuppence a ton, you know. I'll not be long.

Alice exits L

There is a moment of silence as the two men gaze at the door

Sam (*quietly*) Sorry about that, Joe.

Joe No—no. Don't worry yourself, Sam. It's just that—well—I hope you don't think—well—you know—about the meals . . .

Sam Eh? No—no. Of course not.

Joe (*after a slight pause*) I don't know how you put up with it, Sam. Honest I don't.

Sam (*joking*) Listen who's talking. Your Renee led you a dog's life when she were alive.

Joe (*smiling*) Aye—she did that. Still—I've got to be honest about it, Sam. We had a good marriage.

Sam Eh?

Joe Oh, aye. There were nowt wrong with our *marriage*. The trouble started after we'd *left* the church. She had her views on how to run things, and I had mine. So in the end we had to come to a compromise— and we did things her way. Still—it all turned out for the best. Thirty-seven years and never a cross word exchanged.

Sam (*sitting on the sofa*) Now come off it, Joe. I'm not having that. I've heard her yelling at you for hours on end.

Joe I said exchanged, Sam. Exchanged. She never had her mouth shut long enough for me to interrupt. (*He sits beside Sam*)

Sam (*sighing*) Sounds a bit like Alice.

Joe (*thoughtfully*) You know—I've often wondered what she were think-about—that last morning.

Sam How do you mean?

Joe Well—it were sort of funny, like. There she was, laid out in bed and stiff as a board—with a smile all over her face. First time in years I'd seen her smiling. Only thing I could think of was happen she didn't know she were dead.

Sam Gerrout, you daft beggar.

Joe It were strange at first—after she'd gone. I couldn't get used to the silence—it were sort of unnerving. That's when I started going over to the *Commercial* for a pint or two. It made all the difference. She'd never let me touch the stuff before—but by heck—I've been making up for it ever since.

Sam I wish I could. You know, Joe—there's some nights I think I could go mad for the want of a pint. Used to be a big drinker, I did, in the old days. But—well—I take one look at Alice's face . . . (*He shakes his head*)

Joe It's too late for that now, Sam. You should have taken a closer look at it before you marched her up the aisle.

Sam (*sighing*) You'd never believe a lass could change as quick as she did. Sweetness and light one day—and the next . . . (*He sighs again*)

Joe Tell you what. Hows about you and me slipping off for a quick one after you get back from the cemetery?

Sam Sorry, Joe. I daren't risk it. If Alice ever found out she'd go through the roof. You know how she feels about drinking.

Joe How would she know? She'll be going over Half Acres to their Doris's, won't she? Like she does every Saturday night.

Sam Well—aye—I suppose so.

Joe Suppose so, nothing. She's never missed a Saturday at her sisters since old Dan died—'cepting that time she were having your Terry. Come on, Sam. What's to stop you?

Sam (*hesitant*) What about me breath, though? She's bound to smell it on me breath.

Joe Has tha never heard of peppermints, Sam? Just suck a couple of them before tha comes home again, and nobody'll be any the wiser.

Sam (*almost convinced*) Are you sure?

Joe 'Course I'm sure.

Sam (*deciding*) Right then. You're on.

Joe (*delighted*) That's the ticket. (*He rises*) I'll nip up to Wilkinson's right now and buy a packet.

Sam (*rising*) And I'd better get buttering that bread. I'll see you out, Joe.

Sam and Joe exit L. *As they do so, the door* R *opens quietly, and Mabel Sutton slides into the room*

(*Off*) Mind yourself crossing the road.

Mabel quickly poses herself by the sofa

Sam enters L *and sees her*

(*Startled*) Oh.

Mabel Alice about?

Sam Er—no. She's—er—she's just gone up to the chip shop to get the dinner.

Mabel Oh.

Sam (*worried*) You—er—you've just come in, have you? Through the back?

Mabel That's right, Sam.

Sam Oh—it's just that I didn't hear you.

Mabel No. No, I don't suppose you would do. I can be very quiet when I want to be. Is—er—is she likely to be long, do you think?

Sam Depends on how many there are in there, I suppose. Why?

Mabel (*shrugging*) Just wondered, that's all. I—er—I've got something to tell her. Bit of news.

Sam Oh, aye. And what might that be?

Mabel Well—that'd be telling, wouldn't it, Sam?

Sam I bet it's bad news for somebody.

Mabel (*smiling*) You might be right at that, Sam. It could be *very* bad news for *somebody*.

Sam (*sitting on the sofa*) And what's that supposed to mean?

Mabel Anything you'd like it to. Anything you'd like it to mean at all.

Sam You know—that's what I like about you, Mabel. Nothing.

Mabel (*stung*) I beg your pardon.

Sam You're about as subtle as a ton of bricks on the big toe, you are. Come on. Out with it. What nasty little rumour have you got tucked away inside that poisonous mind of yours this time?

Mabel You want to be careful who you're talking to like that, Sam Early. I haven't come round here to be insulted, you know.

Sam Oh? So where do you usually go?

Mabel (*tartly*) I shall ignore that remark. But I'll tell you this much for nothing. There's going to be some right fun and games going off in this house when Alice finds out what's been going on behind her back.

Sam (*startled*) Eh?

Mabel Yes. I thought that'd make you sit up and take notice.

Sam What are you talking about?

Mabel You'll see.

Sam If you're referring to our Terry and young Susan Rickworth . . .

Mabel I'm not.

Sam Then what *are* you getting at?

Mabel Does the word "peppermints" mean anything to you?

Sam Peppermints? Why should . . . (*He realizes*) Oh, lor . . .

Mabel Thought you could sneak off for a night's boozing with Joe Gittings while she were out at her sisters, did you? Well—I'm sure she'll be very interested to hear *that* little snippet—don't you think?

Sam (*rising*) Do you mean you were listening out there—in the passage?

Mabel I did happen to overhear—yes.

Sam Well you nosey old . . .

Mabel It's no use resorting to insults, Sam Early, because they'll just roll off my back like water off a duck. I've not lived in this street for the last thirty-two years without developing a thick skin. No—you might as well just save your breath and start thinking of what you're going to give your Alice by way of an explanation.

Sam (*worried*) Now look—Mabel . . .

Mabel Oh. It's Mabel now, is it? Music box's playing another kind of tune.

Sam It's just a quiet night out—for a drink or two. There's no need for Alice to find out about it, is there?

Mabel Isn't there?

Sam I—er—I could make it worth your while.

Mabel (*sternly*) Are you trying to bribe me?

Sam Well . . .

Mabel Are you trying to persuade me to keep my mouth shut in return for financial gain?

Sam Mabel . . .

Mabel That makes it even worse, Sam Early. Your wife happens to be a very dear friend of mine, and I couldn't sleep in my bed at night with the stench of bribery in my nostrils. My conscience wouldn't allow it.

Sam Oh, all right, then. Forget it. Tell her about it and be damned.

Mabel How much are you offering?

Sam Eh?

Mabel I said how much is it worth?

Sam (*delighted*) You mean you'll do it? Keep it dark? (*Relieved*) Oh, thanks, Mabel. I'll never forget this.

Mabel (*smiling*) I'm not an unreasonable woman, Sam. Not by a long chalk. But I'm not a woman with a short memory either. You've said some very nasty things about me in the past. Things that a lot of

women would hold against you as a grudge. But not me. Not Mabel
Sutton. You see—I know that half the things you've said about me
were said in—well—a kind of *joking* manner, wouldn't you say?

Sam (*eager*) Aye, aye. That's right, Mabel. Just in a joking manner.

They both laugh rather falsely

Mabel Well . . . I'm not going to let anybody say that I haven't got a sense
of humour. I can enjoy a joke as good as anybody else, I can.

They both laugh again

So shall we say three pounds?

Sam (*startled*) Eh? Nay, Mabel—see reason, can't you? Where am I
going to get three pounds from? Alice has care of all the money in this
house. You know that.

Mabel You have your problems, Sam, and I've got mine. Our Eustace is
out of work again, and I can do with a bit of extra cash to help out the
Social Security. Where you get the money from is entirely up to you.

Sam I'll give you an I O U.

Mabel Cash.

Sam But, Mabel . . .

Mabel Cash.

Sam This is blackmail.

Mabel Call it what you will, but if you want my silence, Sam Early, you're
going to have to pay for it.

Alice (*off*) Clear off, you mucky little devils. Go play outside your own
houses.

Mabel Well? Do I get it, or don't I?

Sam (*desperately*) I haven't got it.

The door L *flies open and Alice marches in fuming. She carries a news-
paper parcel of fish and chips*

Alice Filthy little animals. Want dumping in a bath of disinfectant, the
lot of 'em. (*She sees Mabel*) Oh—so you're here are you? (*She moves to
the table*) And what do you want to borrow this time? (*She dumps the
parcel on a plate*)

Mabel I've not come to borrow anything.

Alice (*sniffing*) That makes a change. (*She turns*) Well? What do you want
then? And make it quick—the chips'll be going cold. (*To Sam*) I thought
I told you to get some bread done?

Sam Aye—well . . .

Mabel I came round here with a bit of news I thought you might like to
hear.

Sam winces

Alice Oh? And what's that? (*To Sam*) Where is it? The bread?

Sam I've not had time . . .

Alice Not had time? I've been up to the fish shop and back. (*She grumbles*)

If you want a job doing, do it yourself. (*She marches to the door* R)
Well, go on. I'm listening.

Alice exits

Mabel (*raising her voice*) It's about tonight—when you go out.
Alice (*off*) What about it?

Mabel looks at Sam quizzically, and he shakes his head with frantic pleading

Mabel (*a trifle louder*) Well—I happened to overhear a conversation
between certain parties—quite by accident, you understand—about the
poss——

Mabel is interrupted by a loud cry from Alice, off

Alice (*off*) Oh, no! That's *all* I needed, Sam Early, I could choke you.

Alice enters R

Didn't you know that kettle were boiling itself dry? It's ruined, you've
burnt the elements right out of it.
Sam Eh?
Alice (*blazing*) That's just about the last straw this morning. I've a good
mind to—oh, what's the use of talking. It goes straight in at one ear
and out the other. Get in there and open the window and let some of
that stench out. It's enough to turn your stomach.

Sam begins to move kitchenwards

No. On second thoughts, you'd better leave it to me. Let you near it
and we'll probably be needing a new window as well. Take your hook
up the road and buy a new kettle. (*She takes off her coat and drapes it
over the settee*) And make it snappy. I want a cup of tea with my dinner.
Sam (*glancing at Mabel*) But—er—what about the chips?
Alice Never mind about them. I'll put 'em in the oven till you get back.
Now look sharp. (*She picks up the chip parcel*)
Sam I've got no money, love. You've not give me me allowance yet.
Alice (*putting the chips down again and picking up her purse*) Here—take
this. (*She gives him a ten-pound note*) And don't forget the change.
(*She picks up the parcel again*)

Alice exits R

Mabel (*sweetly*) You'd better get a move on, Sam. They'll be closing for
dinner in a few minutes.
Sam Mabel . . .
Mabel It's still the same price.
Sam Oh—all right. Don't breath a word to Alice and you'll get your
money.
Mabel When?

Sam As soon as I've got some change.

Mabel Better make it quick, Sam. I can't hang on to this bit of information too long, now can I? It's what you might call perishable.

Alice enters R

Alice Haven't you gone yet?

Sam (*backing to the door*) Just going, love.

Alice Well *move* then! (*To Mabel*) Well?

Mabel Well what?

Alice (*patiently*) What's this bit of news you can't wait to tell me?

Mabel Oh—the news. Yes—well—it's nothing very exciting, Alice. It's just that I overheard these two women talking about—er—er—the—er—the bus strike that's due to start tonight.

Sam smiles with relief and exits L

Alice Bus strike? Tonight? That's the first *I've* heard of it.

Mabel Me as well. I couldn't believe me ears.

Alice I bet that came as a shock. You're only too willing to believe 'em for most of the time. Anyway, it's all a load of rubbish. If there were any bus strikes planned for this district, I'd be one of the first to know.

Mabel Oh?

Alice You haven't forgotten our Ethel works for the West Riding, have you?

Mabel (*annoyed with herself*) Oh, of course. I expect they were mistaken then—these two men.

Alice I thought you said they were women?

Mabel Oh, yes. I mean women. (*She laughs falsely*) You can't tell 'em apart, these days, can you?

Alice (*drily*) So it seems.

Mabel (*changing the subject*) So—er—so what's happening about your Terry and that Rickworth girl, then?

Alice Nothing's happening.

Mabel You mean—the wedding's off?

Alice It was never on, so it can hardly be off, can it? When I think it's time for our Terry to get himself wed, then I'll let him know. But till that time comes, he's going to have nothing to do with the hard-faced little trollops around this district.

Mabel (*bridling*) I hope you're not including my Denise in that statement, Alice Early.

Alice And why's she so important she should be left out?

Mabel (*indignantly*) There's nothing of the trollop about *my* daughter.

Alice I wouldn't be too sure about that. I saw her trotting off into town last night with her face painted up like a streetwalker's. And as for that blouse she had on—well—I've seen more cotton in the top of an aspirin bottle.

Mabel (*defensively*) It's the latest fashion.

Alice (*snorting*) Fashion. If they told these young lasses nowadays that a slab of horse muck were the latest fashion, they'd all be rushing to queue up for some.

Mabel (*trying to pass it off*) Well—I expect we were just as bad when we were their age, eh?

Alice You speak for yourself. *I* were always dressed the way a young woman were supposed to dress—and in no other way. My parents saw to it that I were brought up the same way that they were. Clean, neat, tidy, and respectful to their elders. Chapel every Sunday—morning and evening—and all day Good Fridays. When were the last time your two showed their face inside a place of worship? When you had 'em christened?

Mabel Well things are different today, Alice. Besides—we're all Church of England, so it doesn't matter so much for us.

Alice That's obvious.

Mabel Well we might not be first in line when it comes to showing off new clothes and sitting in front pews so's everybody can gawp at us, but we're just as good a Christian as them that does. And I'll tell you this much for nothing, Alice Early. Our Denise might dress up a bit showy like for round here, but she's managed to keep herself chaste this last nineteen years.

Alice Yes—and how often has she been caught?

Mabel Well—really!

Alice She's just like the rest of 'em, is your Denise. Out for a good time and doesn't care how she has it. (*She goes to the window*) Where is he with that kettle?

Mabel If you weren't a friend of mine, Alice Early, I'd walk straight out of this house after a remark like that.

Alice (*peering out*) You needn't let the ties of friendship hold you back. If the truth hurts too much, you know where to find the door.

Mabel (*undecided as to what to do*) I've got half a mind . . . (*She stops*)

Alice (*turning*) Well at least you've got the good grace to admit that much. (*She goes to the door* R) Them chips'll be frizzled to a cinder if he doesn't hurry himself up. (*Suddenly turning back to Mabel*) You're not using your kettle for the minute, are you?

Mabel Well . . .

Alice Good. I'll borrow that then. You can go out the back way, but watch where you're putting your feet. I only did that doorstep this morning.

Mabel It's not a modern kettle, you know, Alice.

Alice That's all right, Mabel. I want to boil water in it, not admire it. Come on. I'll let you through.

Alice and Mabel exit R. *After a moment the door* L *opens and Terry comes in to slump on the sofa in utter dejection Alice returns, marching in* R *with a plate of bread and a butter-dish*

(*Moving to the table*) Oh—so you've decided to come back, have you? And just where do you think you've been?

Terry (*morosely*) Out.

Alice (*slamming the bread and butter down on the table*) If you use that tone of voice to me again, Terry Early, I'll rattle your earhole for you. I asked you where you'd been.

Terry I've told you. I went out. Up the street.

Alice Running after her.

Terry No.

Alice Don't lie to me. I saw you.

Terry I wasn't. I just wanted to think things over, that's all.

Alice What things?

Terry Me and Susan.

Alice *And??*

Terry And what?

Alice What great decision did you come to?

Terry (*quietly*) I haven't made me mind up, yet.

Alice Well you needn't strain your mental resources any longer. I've made the decision for you. You'll not see that girl again and that's the end of it. (*Buttering the bread*) Now go get yourself washed and come and get your dinner.

Terry rises slowly

And while you're about it, you can get yourself out of them trousers and put yourself into a decent pair. Them things are so tight, folks can tell your religion.

Terry But Mum, I'm going out this afternoon.

Alice All the more reason for covering yourself up.

Terry I'm going out on me motorbike.

Alice You're doing nothing of the kind. You're coming with me and your dad up to the cemetery.

Terry Mum . . .

Alice There's a clean shirt in your drawer. And not one of them coloured ones. A white one's more respectful to the dead.

Terry But I've promised, Mum. I'm meeting the lads at two.

Alice You're meeting nobody at no time. You're coming with us, and that's final. I'll keep you respectable if it kills me.

Mabel enters R *carrying a very battered electric kettle with a frayed flex*

Mabel I've got it. But you'll have to go careful though. It's a bit on the wonky side.

Alice (*taking it from her*) Took you long enough, didn't it?

Terry exits L

Mabel Well, our Eustace was using it. He was shaving, you see.

Alice Oh . . . he's managed to borrow a razor blade from somebody, has he?

Alice exits R *with the kettle*

Mabel (*glaring after her*) Honestly, some folks. (*She calls*) Be careful how much you put in it, Alice. It's a bit funny sometimes. You have to cover the element, you know. But not too much or else it starts to throw sparks out when it's boiling.

Alice (*off*) I have used an electric kettle before.

Mabel (*shrugging*) Well, I'm only telling you.

Alice enters R

Alice I suppose you'll be staying for a cup?

Mabel opens her mouth, but Alice sweeps on

I thought as much. (*She goes to the sideboard for another cup and saucer*) And that reminds me—you still owe me a quarter of tea from last week—and two eggs.

Mabel Oh aye—that's right. I'd not forgotten.

Alice No. And neither had I. (*She puts the cup and saucer on the table*)

Mabel Mind you—it's the kind of thing that one *could* forget quite easy, isn't it? I mean for somebody in *my* position.

Alice Oh? And what's your position?

Mabel Well—being a widow with two children. It's not the easiest thing in the world, Alice.

Alice I don't see as how it's any different from what it was when your Fred were still around, except you've got one less mouth to feed. He didn't do a day's work in the twenty-five years I knew him.

Mabel Well, he had his heart trouble, didn't he? He couldn't do much with a complaint like that. And anyway—there's nobody can say as he didn't *want* to work. Look at that morning he died. Right there in the Labour Exchange, he was when his heart give out.

Alice Yes. Just after they'd found him a job.

Mabel fumes

Sam enters L *with a box*

Sam I've got one. (*He looks at Mabel*)

Alice I thought you were making it the time it took you. Anyway, I've borrowed hers, so you can put that down and go wash yourself.

Sam puts the box down on the sideboard

And while you're at it, you can tell our Terry to get a move on. I'm putting the dinner out now.

Alice exits R

Mabel Well? Did you get the change? (*She holds her hand out*)

Sam Eh? Oh—aye . . . (*He fishes in his pocket and brings out two pound notes*) There's two here, and I'll have to give you the other one later.
Mabel All right, then—but don't forget—or else.

Terry enters L. *He is now dressed in neat trousers, and slip-on shoes. His torso is naked and he carries a white shirt in his hand*

(*With arch delight*) Oh, look at Tarzan here.

Terry scowls at her and moves below the sofa

Alice enters R *with the chip parcel*

Alice (*spotting Terry*) What are you doing running round half naked. Put your shirt on. (*She goes to the table*)
Terry It's got a button missing.
Alice Then put one on that hasn't. (*She puts the chips down*)
Terry You said a white one. All my others are coloured. (*He sits on the sofa arm*)
Alice (*fuming*) Men. (*She crosses to him and takes the shirt*) Get over there and eat your dinner while I do it for you. One of these days *I* might get a hot meal if I'm lucky.
Mabel Would you like me to do it for him, Alice? (*She gets hold of the shirt*)
Alice No thank you. I'd sooner it were done properly.
Sam Oh, go on, Alice. Let her do it for you, and you come and have your dinner. (*He moves above the table by the parcel*)
Mabel (*needled*) Not if you don't think I'm good enough.
Alice (*after a moment's indecision*) I'll get you the needle and cotton. (*She goes to the sideboard drawer and rummages in it*)
Sam Come on, Terry. (*He begins to unwrap the chip parcel*)
Terry I don't want anything, thanks. I'm not hungry.

Sam stops what he is doing

Alice (*turning*) Sit down at that table and do as you're told. I'm not wasting good money on food so that you can turn your nose up at it. (*She brings out cotton and needle*)

Terry moves silently to the table and sits. Alice hands the sewing things to Mabel, who sits on the sofa with the shirt

Mabel That kettle should be boiling by now. (*She begins to thread the needle*)
Alice And not before time. I'd have done better with a couple of candles under the other one.
Mabel Well I did warn you, didn't I? It's an old one.
Alice (*to Sam*) Don't just stand there staring at 'em. They won't unwrap themselves, you know.
Terry (*turning in his chair*) Why can't me and Susan get engaged? What's wrong with *her*?

Alice Get your dinner.

Terry I'm asking you a fair question, Mother. What's wrong with Susan?

Alice Never you mind what's wrong with her. You're not going to marry her, and that's final.

Terry Well that's where you're one off, because I *am* going to marry her. No matter what you or the flaming magistrates' court has to say about it, so you can stick that in your pipe and smoke it.

Alice Don't you talk to me like that, Terry Early.

Terry I'll talk to you any way I like. I'm sick and tired of you telling me what I can and can't do. (*He rises*) I'm seventeen years old, mother, and I'm going to make my own decisions in future—and the first thing I've decided is I'm going to buy an engagement ring for Susan this afternoon and I'm not going up to that bloody cemetery.

Alice (*her eyes blazing*) You are not buying an engagement ring for that girl this afternoon, Terry Early. Not this afternoon or any other. Not by *any* stretch of the imagination, you aren't.

Terry Just you try and stop me.

Mabel (*anxiously*) Alice. The kettle. It'll be sparking.

Alice (*ignoring her*) You'll buy that engagement ring over my dead body. (*She moves to the door* R) Do you hear? Over my dead body.

Alice exits R

There is a deathly silence. Terry sits again. Sam begins to unwrap the chips. Mabel looks down at her sewing. There is a loud scream from Alice off. Everybody looks up, startled

Mabel (*rising*) The kettle . . .

Sam (*rising*) Eh?

Mabel It's got a fault in it. I warned her.

Sam (*calling*) Alice! Alice! (*He hurries to the door* R) Are you all right?

Sam exits R

Mabel (*panic-stricken*) I told her it was faulty. I did tell her.

Sam (*off*) Alice! (*Louder*) Alice . . .!

There is a silence. Mabel looks at Terry

Mabel Go and see what's happened.

Terry makes no move

Quick—she might need a doctor.

Terry still makes no move

Don't just *stand* there.

Terry (*looking at her*) It's all right—she'll be all right.

Mabel (*insistent*) Go find out.

The door R *opens slowly and Sam stands there, his face blank*

Mabel and Terry stare at him

   (*Suddenly*) Well? What's happened? Is she all right?

Sam is silent

   Say something, can't you?
Sam (*to Terry, quietly*) Looks like you'll be able to buy that ring after all,
   lad.

*Terry stares at Sam in disbelief. Mabel gives a soft moan and collapses on the
sofa, as—*

the CURTAIN falls

SCENE 2

The same. The following Saturday evening

When the CURTAIN *rises, the room is empty and in darkness. The heavy
curtains at the windows are drawn, and only a faint glow from the fire
penetrates the blackness. After a moment, the sound of voices in the street
begins to make itself known. It is Sam and Joe, who in drunken tones are
singing "Two o'clock in the morning". The voices come closer, then the
clatter of milk bottles rings out as they are kicked over*

Joe (*off*) Hey up.
Sam (*off*) Milk-o.

They laugh. The clatter of bottles breaks out again

Mabel (*off*) What's going on down there? What do you think you're play-
   ing at?
Sam ⎫
Joe ⎬ (*off*) Meowwwwwwwww Meowwwwwwww. ⎱(*Speaking together
        ⎭   ⎰ and laughing*)
Mabel (*off*) Is that you down there, Sam Early? Is that you?
Sam (*off*) Soft—what light in yonder window breaks? Tis Mabel. Frosty
   faced old Mabel.
Mabel (*off*) I'll give you frosty faced, you drunken pig. Take that!

   *There is a loud yell from the men. A clatter of bottles. Then the sound of
   the front door bursting open. Sam and Joe emerge through the door* L,
   *Sam turning on the light as he enters. Both have wet shoulders and hair.
   They look at each other and giggle happily*

Joe Here—I hope that weren't what I thought it were. (*He wipes at his
   shoulder*)
Sam So do I. (*He sniffs at his own shoulder*) Pooh—it were! Cor blimey—I
   wish she'd change the water in that flower vase more often. (*He takes
   his jacket off and hangs it on a chair back*)

Joe (*taking his jacket off*) What did she want to go and do a thing like that for? Miserable owd devil. (*He drapes his coat on the sofa back*)

Sam (*moving to the window*) She must be one of them folks what don't like Shakespeare, Joe. (*He sniggers*) Still—never mind. So long as it didn't get into the beer. (*He dries his hair on the curtains*)

Joe (*grinning*) No fear o' that, Sam. (*He pulls a bottle of beer out from each of his jacket pockets*) Safe as houses.

There is a loud knocking off R

Mabel (*off*) Sam Early! Sam Early!
Joe Aye aye.
Sam Sounds like Juliet's come down from her balcony.

The knocking comes again

All right, all right, hold your horses. I'm coming. (*He moves up to the door* L) Hide them bottles, Joe. We don't want the ale to go flat when she pokes her face in.

Sam exits L

Joe hides the bottles under the sofa cushions

Mabel (*off*) What do you mean by waking folks up at this time of night? Eh? Don't you think we've got enough noise going on during the day-time without you shouting and bawling your head off at a quarter to one in the morning. Some folks are trying to get a decent night's sleep, some folks are.
Man's Voice (*off*) Quiet down, there, can't you?
Mabel (*off*) Quiet yourself!
Man (*off*) Drunken old cat!
Mabel (*off*) Don't you call me a drunken old cat, Bert Stebbins!
Woman's Voice (*off*) Make less noise down there!
Mabel (*off*) You keep your nose out of things that don't concern you!
Man (*off*) Quiet!
Woman (*off*) Clear off!
Mabel (*off*) Clear off yourself!
Sam (*off, singing*) The street is alive—with the sound of voices.
Voices (*off*) Quiet! Make less noise! Shut that racket!
Mabel (*off*) Now see what you've done, Sam Early. You've woken the whole flaming street up.
Voices (*off*) Quiet! Shut up!

Mabel enters L. *She is dressed in an old flannelette nightdress topped by an even older and grubby looking dressing gown. Her hair is in rollers and covered by a chiffon scarf, and her face is shiny with cream. She wears slippers*

The voices are cut off as Sam closes the door off

Mabel (*spotting Joe*) Oh—so you're here as well, are you? I might have known it.

Joe Blimey! It's the new Miss World.

Sam enters L, *closing the door behind him*

Mabel You ought to be ashamed of yourself—the both of you. Look at you. Just look at you. Well, all I can say, Sam Early, is thank goodness poor Alice isn't here to see what you get up to when she's out of the way. Just one week—that's all it is. Just one week since she fell down dead in that kitchen, and here you are, drunk as lords and acting like—like—I don't know what. (*To Sam*) If your Alice knew what condition you were in at this minute, she'd scratch her way up out of her grave and throttle you.

Sam She'd have a job on. I had her cremated. (*He laughs*)

Mabel Yes—you can laugh, Sam Early. But I don't know how you can sleep nights having what you've done this last week on your conscience.

Sam And what's that?

Mabel I'll tell you what that is, Mr Clever-know-it-all Early. Your conscience is a little thing that keeps nagging away at you all night and all day.

Joe That's best bit of self-description I've heard in a long time. (*He laughs*)

Mabel You keep your trap shut. There's a bus coming.

Sam I didn't mean that, Mabel. I meant what *have* I got on my conscience?

Mabel Well, if you don't know, I'm certainly not going to tell you.

Sam Good.

Mabel There's your Terry for a start.

Sam What about him?

Mabel What about him? I'll tell you what about him.

Joe (*tiredly*) I thought she would.

Mabel Getting himself engaged to that Rickworth girl and *then* having the brass face to put it in the *Express* before his mother's poor body had time to go cold. How that woman can rest quiet I just don't know. I just *don't* know.

Sam (*nodding*) Aye—aye, you've got something there, Mabel. I don't know either, come to think of it.

Mabel (*self-satisfied*) Oh . . . so you do have *some* thought for the dear departed, then?

Sam (*frowning*) It never struck me before. I never thought on. But it's just come to me. Somewhere up there—(*he indicates heaven*)—or more likely down there—(*he indicates the floor*)—poor old Alice must be watching us. Me out every night getting sozzled, and our Terry engaging himself to the last girl in the world she wanted him to marry. Both of us enjoying life more than we ever have done over the last nineteen years, and her not being able to do a thing to stop us. (*He shakes his head in sorrow*) She'll be as frustrated as hell. (*He lets out a huge bellow of laughter and slaps Joe's back*)

Mabel (*shocked*) Oh!

Sam And now let *me* tell *you* something, Mrs Mabel-nosy-Sutton. *I'm* the boss in this house now, and if I want to go out for a few drinks with my pal on my anniversary, then I *shall* do. And neither you nor anybody else is going to stop me. Understand?

Joe (*fishing out the bottles*) That's right, Sam. You tell her.

Mabel Anniversary? What anniversary? You were married in July.

Sam I'm not talking about me wedding anniversary. I've spent the last eighteen years trying to forget that. I'm talking about my FREEDOM anniversary. It's exactly one week today since Alice Louise Early went to that better place she were always preaching about—and if *that's* not something to celebrate, then I don't know what is.

Mabel Oh—you disgust me, Sam Early. Utterly *disgust* me.

Sam Maybe I do—but then—you didn't have to live with her, did you? No, it were me what had to put up with her bossing and organizing, day in and day out, not you. You didn't have to suffer like I did.

Mabel Suffer? What do you mean, suffer? She were a good wife to you were your Alice. Far better than you deserved.

Sam Perhaps so. I've never claimed to be perfect.

Mabel It's a good job, an' all. You'd have been sued under the Trades Description Act.

Joe Oh, cut the cackle and take your hook, Mabel.

Mabel (*to Joe*) And we'll have less chelp from you, while we're at it. I blame you for all this lot, Joe Gittings. If you hadn't persuaded him to sneak off for a quick booze-up, poor Alice'd still be with us.

Joe Don't you come blaming me, Mabel Sutton. It were your kettle what did the job, not mine.

Mabel Yes—but if he hadn't let theirs burn its bottom out, she'd never have borrowed mine.

Joe Aye. But she did. And like that coroner chap said at the inquest . . . you should have had more sense than to lend somebody summat as dangerous as that kettle was.

Mabel (*on the defence*) What did he know about it? She *made* me lend it her. *You* know that. What right had *he* got to say things like that about me—her best friend?

Sam Best friend me foot. You were scared stiff of her like all the rest of us. Licking her hand every time she kicked you. (*With sudden inspiration*) It wouldn't surprise me if you didn't lend her that kettle on a purpose!

Mabel (*horrified*) Oh—Sam Early.

Joe (*with a straight face*) Look at the guilt on her face.

Mabel (*backing*) It's not true—I didn't. (*Dropping to her knees and looking upwards*) Alice—oh, Alice. If you're up there somewhere watching me—I swear I didn't do it on purpose. I swear it.

There is a tremendous crack of thunder which makes them all jump

Sam By heck—that were a close one.

Joe Sounds like we're in for a storm.

Mabel (*scrambling to her feet*) I—I'd best be getting back home. Our Denise isn't so keen on thunder and stuff.

Sam Aye, go on. Take your hook. We've got some bottles here and they're starting to get a bit lonely.

Mabel (*beginning to recover from her shock*) Don't think that this is the last of it, Sam Early. I shall have something else to say to you tomorrow morning about this lot, and don't you think I won't.

The thunder rolls again

Sam Well you needn't bother yourself. Anything you want to say, you can say it now and get it off your chest.

Mabel (*opening the door* L) I said tomorrow. I'll bite me tongue till then.

Joe I shouldn't do that if I were you, Mabel. You might give yourself blood poisoning.

Sam and Joe laugh

Mabel turns in a huff and exits L

Sam Come on, Joe. Get that bottle-opener working.

There is a tremendous crack of thunder which makes them both look up. This is followed by an ear-splitting scream of terror from Mabel

Joe (*startled*) What the . . .
Sam Mabel . . .

Joe and Sam dash for the door L, *collide, rush through, and exit*

The thunder rolls again

Joe (*off*) On the doorstep, Sam.
Sam (*off*) Mabel, Mabel!

After a moment, Joe and Sam enter L, *carrying the limp form of Mabel*

On to the sofa with her, Joe.

They deposit her full length on the sofa

Open one o' them bottles and give her a swig of ale. Happen it'll bring her round. (*He kneels beside her*)

Joe locates a bottle-opener and begins to take off the bottle-cap, moving behind the sofa

Joe I wonder what happened to her? She's not been struck, has she?
Sam No—no. (*Patting her cheeks*) Must have been that last clap of thunder. (*He pats her cheek again*) She's out cold.
Joe (*frowning down at her*) First time in years I've seen her with her mouth shut. (*He holds the bottle out to Sam*)
Mabel (*moaning*) Ohhhhhh.

Sam (*leaning over her*) It's all right, Mabel. It's all right.

Mabel (*springing bolt upright*) No—no. (*She screams*) Noooooooooooo!

Sam (*startled*) Hey—hey . . .

Mabel (*frantically*) Keep her away from me. Keep her away. (*She screams*)

Joe (*trying to calm her*) Hold on a minute. Hold on. What's up with you, woman?

Mabel (*grabbing Sam*) Save me. Save me. (*She screams again*)

Sam struggles to free himself

Sam Mabel! Gerroff—Mabel . . . (*He yells*) Mabeeeeeel!

Mabel (*snapping out of it*) Eh?

Sam You're choking me. (*He pulls himself free*)

Joe (*putting his hand on her shoulder*) What's to do? No need to go mad, you know. Calm down. Calm down.

Mabel (*dazedly*) Where am I? What's happened?

Sam You're here—in the house. With us. It's all right.

Mabel House? (*She puts her fingers to her temples*)

Sam Aye. We found you on the doorstep.

Joe Lying there like a sack of flour, you were. Good job we heard you yelling, else you'd have caught your death of cold in that rain.

Sam You made enough din to waken the dead.

Mabel suddenly lets out another ear-splitting yell. Sam and Joe jump

Mabel. (*Louder*) Mabel! (*He slaps his hand over her mouth*)

Thunder rolls again

Joe What's up with her?

Mabel (*pulling Sam's hand aside*) Sam . . . she's back. Alice. She's come back.

Sam (*stupidly*) Alice?

Mabel (*urgently*) She was there—in the street—watching me.

Joe looks at Sam, indicates Mabel and taps his temple knowingly

Sam Alice? You mean—*my* Alice?

Mabel (*nodding*) She's come back to haunt us, Sam. To *avenge* herself.

Sam (*uneasily*) Don't talk daft. (*He laughs nervously*)

Mabel (*clutching his arm*) It's true. I could tell it by the look on her face. I could *see* it in her eyes. (*She wails*) Oh, Sam.

Joe Shut your snivelling, woman. There's no such things as ghosts. You must have been seeing things.

Mabel I wasn't. She was there. Outside in the rain.

Sam Did—did she say anything? You know—speak to you?

Mabel Not a word—she just stood there glaring——

Joe Glaring but not speaking?

Mabel nods

Sam (*sighing with relief*) That's all right then. It couldn't have been Alice.

Mabel (*insistent*) But it *was*. I could see right through her. She was standing by the railings across the road. It was horrible.

Joe You couldn't have done. It's pitch black out there. You can't see the edge of the pavement, never mind across the road.

Mabel It was in the lightning.

The two men look at each other again

Sam Happen we'd best go and take a look, Joe? Maybe somebody were playing a joke?

Joe Aye . . .

Mabel It were no joke, Sam. You can't mistake a thing like that.

Joe I'll go. You stay here and try to talk a bit of sense into her. Ghosts.

Joe exits L

There is another loud crash of thunder

Mabel She *was* there, Sam.

Sam Aye.

There is a short silence. Mabel pulls her dressing gown closer to her. Sam glances sideways at her

Mabel You—er—you wouldn't have a drop of—brandy or anything, would you, Sam? Just to settle me?

Sam No. Alice wouldn't . . . (*He remembers the beer*) There's a drop of light ale. (*He offers the bottle*)

Mabel (*taking it*) Thanks, Sam. (*She drinks*)

Sam Look—Mabel—you don't think that—well—that you could have made a *mistake*? I mean—well—*ghosts*?

Mabel (*shaking her head*) There was no mistake. She was there, Sam. Just like I told you. All lit up in the lightning. (*She drinks again*)

Sam But . . . (*He shrugs helplessly*) She *couldn't* have been.

There is another short silence, broken only by a long rumble of thunder. Sam sits beside Mabel

How did she look?

Mabel (*shuddering*) I don't want to talk about it. (*She drinks*)

Sam Oh.

Mabel (*suddenly*) She was all transparent and shiny.

Sam Shiny?

Mabel (*eyes wide*) Like glass. With the rain falling right through her. Right through her—and I could see the railings as well—all black and wet—like bones dripping with blood . . .

Sam (*gulping*) Blood?

Mabel And her arms—waving up and down at me—like this. (*She waves her arms energetically*) Up and down. Up and down.

Sam And then what happened?

Mabel I screamed and fainted. (*She takes another long swig at the bottle*)

Sam (*glancing over his shoulder*) I wonder what's keeping Joe? P'raps I'd better go have a look. (*He rises*)

Mabel (*terrified*) No—don't leave me here on me own. She might be hovering around somewhere. (*She looks around fearfully*)

Sam You'll be all right. (*He turns to the door* L)

The door begins to open slowly. A transparent shape appears in the opening, dripping with water

Sam staggers backwards, falling over the sofa arm and on to Mabel. Mabel sees the shape and lets out an ear-splitting shriek

The shape enters. It is Joe, behind a large polythene sheet

Joe (*lowering the sheet*) Hold your noise, woman. Hold your noise.

Sam (*struggling to his feet*) Joe . . .

Joe Here's your flaming ghost. A lump of polythene sheeting wrapped round the palings. (*He drops it to the floor*) Stupid old faggot.

Mabel (*gaping*) Polythene sheeting? (*She rises*)

Sam (*starting to laugh*) I might have guessed it. I might have guessed.

Joe It must have blown over from the railway sidings, and got itself hooked.

Mabel You mean—that's all it was? Just that? (*She points*)

Joe Course it was, you daft beggar. (*He snorts*) Ghosts. You'll be asking us to believe in Santa Claus next.

Mabel (*staring at the sheeting*) But—it waved at me.

Joe It were flapping in the wind.

Sam (*chortling*) If you could only see your face, Mabel.

Mabel (*pulling herself together*) Yes, and if *you* could only see *yours*, Sam Early. It'd give you something else to laugh at. (*She wiggles her shoulders*) Go on, laugh. I'm only a poor defenceless widow woman, I am. Have a good laugh at me.

Joe Oh, I wouldn't say you were defenceless, Mabel. Not with a face like yours.

Mabel Oh, very funny, Joe Gittings. Very funny indeed. But you'd have been laughing on the other side of your face if it *had* been Alice out there, wouldn't you? Yes. It'd have been a different carry-on then, wouldn't it?

Sam I'll say it would, Mabel. If it *had* been Alice, and she'd seen you like that—(*he indicates her attire*)—I reckon it'd have been *her* that fainted.

Mabel Yes—you can sneer—but you've got a lot to answer for when that woman meets up with you again. (*To Joe*) And that goes for you as well.

Sam (*cheerfully*) Never mind, Mabel, me old love. We can always pray for salvation at the eleventh hour, can't we?

Mabel I suppose you can, but while you're doing it, you might as well remember that them as does so—often dies at *ten thirty*. Anyway, I've said enough for one night, so I'm off back to me bed, and this time I'd appreciate it if you'd keep your racket to yourselves.

Joe (*brightly*) Good night, Mabel.

Mabel moves to the door L *then turns*

Mabel Isn't somebody going to see me home? You can't expect me to walk round the streets on my own when I'm dressed like this.

Joe You're only going next door.

Mabel That's beside the point. Sam?

Joe It's all right, Sam. I'll do it. (*He moves up to Mabel*) Come on.

Mabel And don't you think just because I'm in my nightclothes, Joe Gittings, that you can come any of your funny stuff with me. I'm particular, I am. (*She opens the door*)

Joe Oh, go on with you, woman. Albert Schweitzer wouldn't touch you, and he touched lepers. Go on. (*He pushes her out*)

Mabel exits, followed by Joe

Sam stoops and picks up the polythene sheet. He grins and begins to fold it

Sam It'll come in handy for the allotment, this will. I'll just pop it into the kitchen.

Sam exits R *with the sheet*

There is another long roll of thunder. The light flickers and goes out, comes on again, then goes out completely, leaving the room in semi-darkness

(*Off*) Oy!

Sam appears in the doorway R *groping for the switch*

Oh, blimey. That's all we needed. The lights have fused.

Sam vanishes from sight again, heading R

(*Off*) Ouch! Owww!

There is silence for a few more seconds, then Terry and Susan enter L. *He is dressed in sweater and slacks. Susan is in skirt and blouse with bolero top, and has his jacket around her*

Terry (*fiddling with the light switch*) Hello? Lights must have gone. (*Shivering*) Cor, what a night. (*He guides Susan to the fireside*))

Susan (*shivering*) I'm soaking. (*She takes Terry's coat off*)

Terry (*taking the coat off her*) You and me both. I'll go see if I can find some towels. You stop here by the fire and get warm.

Susan All right. (*She holds her hands out to the fire*) But don't be long.

Terry I'll try not—providing I can find me way to the airing-cupboard without waking me dad up. (*He shivers*)

Susan (*lowering her voice*) Sorry—I'd forgotten about your dad being asleep.

Terry (*lowering his also*) It's all right. He'll be well away by this time. Won't be a jiffy.

Terry exits

Susan crouches in front of the fire, shivering, for a few moments. She then rises and takes off her bolero top

Susan (*feeling it*) Ugh. (*She lays it on the pouffe to dry out*) Hurry up with those towels. (*She shivers and clutches her shoulders, and edges round to sink down on to the sofa. With much shivering, she draws her legs up on to the sofa beside her*)

Terry enters L *with two large bath-towels*

Terry (*quietly*) Sue?
Susan (*looking round*) Over here. On the sofa.

Terry moves cautiously over to her, holding out one of the towels. Susan takes it gratefully

Thanks. (*She dabs enthusiastically at her arms and face*) Oh, I'm *freezing*!
Terry (*sitting beside her*) We'll soon warm up now we're indoors. (*He rubs at his hair with the towel*) Cor, what a night to miss the last bus.
Susan (*suddenly aware*) Terry—you're drenched. You'll catch your death of cold. Get that sweater off.
Terry Oh, I'm all right.
Susan I'm not having your dad blaming me if you go down with pneumonia. Go on. Change it for something else, and quick.
Terry I can't go crashing round the house in a blackout looking for dry clothing. I might knock something over. Besides, my pants are wet through as well.
Susan Then take *them* off as well.
Terry Aye, aye. Who's wanting a crafty peep at the famous hairy legs of Mr Terence Early, then?
Susan Oh, don't talk so daft. If you think the sight of your bony knees are going to do anything for me, you've got another think coming.
Terry How do you know I've got bony knees?
Susan Because I've sat on them, that's why. Now get those trousers off and wrap a towel round yourself till they dry, else you'll be getting rheumatics and *I'll* have to carry *you* over the threshold.
Terry (*standing*) All right, then. But no peeping.

Susan snorts, and turns her head towards the fire. Terry strips off his sweater and drops it on to the floor. He unfastens his belt, pushes his trousers down to his ankles, then struggles to tug them off over his shoes

Sam enters R, *blindly, arms outstretched. He moves behind Terry and his hand comes in contact with Terry's backside*

Sam lets out a yell. Terry spins round, trousers still round his ankles, and falls into Sam's arms. Susan turns, startled. The lights flash on, off, then on again and stay on. Terry struggles upright

Sam Terry!
Terry Dad.
Susan Hello.

Sam spots Susan for the first time, then gapes at Terry

Terry We thought you were in bed.
Sam (*looking down at Terry's ankles*) Aye . . .

Terry looks down, realizes, and quickly pulls his trousers up again, clutching them to him

Terry (*by way of explanation*) I was just taking my clothes off.
Sam So I noticed.
Susan (*quickly*) It was me that told him to, Mr Early.

Sam looks at Susan

Terry I got wet, you see. We were caught in the rain. Missed the bus, and everything. I'm soaking.
Sam Oh.
Terry All the lights were out and I didn't want to wake you up if you were asleep, so I was getting changed down here. It's all quite innocent, Dad.
Susan (*nodding*) Absolutely.
Terry I was going to fix the fuse as soon as I'd got changed.
Sam Aye. That's what I were trying to do, but it turned out it weren't the fuse at all. Must have been the storm. Anyway—you'd best be getting upstairs and into some dry clothing while you've got chance. There's no telling if they might go off again.
Terry Oh—yes. Righto then. I won't be a jiffy, Sue. (*He backs to the door* L)
Sam (*picking up the sweater*) And you'd better put this somewhere to dry while you're at it. (*He holds it out*)
Terry Oh—yes.

Terry lets go of his trousers to take the sweater, and they begin to fall again. He hurriedly grabs them, and the sweater, and exits L

Susan I hope you don't think . . .
Sam No. No. I don't think anything of the sort, lass. I've never been one for jumping to conclusions. But you must admit it might have looked different to somebody else's eyes.

Susan smiles

Do you fancy something to warm you up? Cocoa, perhaps?
Susan (*gratefully*) I wouldn't mind, Mr Early.
Sam (*moving to the door* R) It's a rough night, isn't it?
Susan I'll say. We had to walk all the way from Lock Lane in it, too.

Sam Lock Lane? What were you doing down there? (*Quickly*) Not that it's anything to do with me where you go, like . . .

Susan (*smiling to show she takes no offence*) We went to Brian Nugent's. You know—Terry's mate from work. He's going to be our best man when—well—when we finally get married.

Sam (*opening the door*) I'm glad you said finally. You've not been engaged five minutes.

Susan Well—it won't be for a long time yet, Mr Early. It's just that we want to get everything sorted out well in advance. And in any case we wouldn't want to get married just yet. I mean—it wouldn't be right—not after—you know . . .

Sam (*puzzled*) Eh? (*He moves down to the back of the sofa*)

Susan With you being in mourning.

Sam Mourning? (*He realizes*) Oh. *Mourning.* Aye—aye—well, you don't have to worry about me. You get married whenever you feel like it. It's your life, and you want to live it the best way you can. (*He shakes his head*) I wish I had *my* time to come all over again. I wouldn't make the same mistakes twice.

Susan Mistakes?

Sam Aye—like getting myself wed before I'd had the chance to enjoy meself.

Susan (*anxiously*) You don't think *we're* rushing things, do you, Mr Early?

Sam No—no. So long as you're sure you've found the right person.

Susan There's no doubt about that, Mr Early. Ours is going to be a marriage made in heaven.

Sam That's what I thought mine was going to be, but it ended up as hell on earth. (*He turns*) I'll go make that cocoa.

Terry enters L *in new trousers and a different sweater*

Terry I'm back. (*He moves to Susan*)

Sam (*at the door*) Would you like some cocoa? I'm just off to make some.

Terry Wouldn't say no. (*He sits on the sofa*)

Sam Won't be long.

Sam exits R

Terry (*flinging his arms around Susan*) Quick. Give us a kiss before he comes back. (*He tries to kiss her*)

Susan (*pushing him away*) Honestly—you men are all the same. Thank goodness. (*She pecks him on the cheek*)

Terry How would you know? Come on. You can do better than that. (*He kisses her properly*)

The door L *opens and Joe enters*

Joe Oops—sorry.

Terry and Susan spring apart

Joe Don't disturb yourself, lad. I've just called back for me coat.

Terry looks round and sees the coat on the sofa back

Terry (*picking it up*) This it?

Joe Aye, that's the one. (*He takes it*) I—er—I'll be off now. G'night, Miss —Terry . . .

Terry Me dad's in the kitchen if you want him. Making cocoa.

Joe No—no. It's all right. I'll see him tomorrow, p'raps.

Sam enters R

Sam Won't be a—— (*He sees Joe*) Oh, hello, Joe. Everything all right, now?

Joe As right as it'll ever be. Silly old beggar.

Terry and Susan look at each other

   Mrs Sutton next door.

Terry Oh?

Sam makes shushing motions to Joe but he fails to see them

Joe Thought she saw a ghost in the street.

Sam grimaces

Susan Ghost?

Terry What sort of ghost?

Joe Your moth—— (*He realizes*) I mean . . .

Terry Mother's ghost? (*He looks at Sam in bewilderment*)

Sam (*quickly*) It were just a sheet of polythene caught on the palings across the road, but she thought it was your mother.

Terry (*laughing*) Come back to haunt us all, I suppose?

Joe If you ask me, it were a guilty conscience. Anyway, I've just taken her back home and left their Eustace looking after her.

Terry But what was she doing out in the street at this time of the night? And in the pouring rain.

Sam Oh, just poking her nose into other folk's business, as usual. P'raps this'll cure her for a while.

Joe Not if I know Mabel Sutton. Anyroad up. I'd best be getting off home. It's nigh on quarter past one.

Susan (*startled*) What? (*She looks at her watch*) No wonder we missed that bus. It's stopped. Oh, Terry, me dad'll kill me, coming in at this time.

Terry (*worried*) We'd better get off straight away then, so I can explain to him.

Susan gets her bolero top

Sam What about your cocoa?

Terry I'll have it when I get back.

Susan (*hurrying to the door* L) Sorry about this, Mr Early, but I just *have* to go.

Sam Aye—all right.
Terry See you later, Dad. G'night, Mr Gittings.

Terry hurries Susan out into the corridor

Joe (*calling*) Take an umbrella with you, lad.
Terry (*off*) Bye.

The door slams off L

Joe Youngsters. I'll go the back way if you don't mind, Sam. It'll be quicker for me.
Sam Aye—aye, 'course. I'll see you out—unless you'd care for a drop of cocoa before you go?
Joe No—no, thanks. Never touch the stuff. (*He moves to the door* R) See thi tomorrow then, Sam. We can try the *George and Dragon* in Bridge Street, happen?
Sam (*following him*) Aye—and I wouldn't mind another go at the *Prince of Wales* in Carleton Street either.

Sam and Joe exit R

There is another crash of thunder and the lights flicker

(*Off*) Good night, Joe.
Joe (*off*) Good night, Sam.

After a moment Sam enters R *with a mug of cocoa*

Sam moves slowly down to the fire. As he reaches it, there is another crack of thunder. The lights flicker and go out

Sam (*groaning*) Oh, not again.

The lights come on again. Sam looks up at the fitting and smiles. He puts down his mug on the mantelpiece and crosses over to the window in front of the sofa. After a slight pause to tidy up the cushions on it, he continues to the window, lifts the curtain and peers out of the window into the night (*Singing softly*) Heaven help the sailors on a night like this. (*He drops the curtain again and moves back towards the fire, crossing behind the sofa. His attention is caught by the framed photo of Alice and himself on their wedding day. Without pausing, he reaches out and turns it to the wall. On reaching the fireplace, he turns slowly and gazes at the picture-frame back. Frowning slightly, he moves back to it, picks it up and looks at the picture thoughtfully. He moves back to the fireplace with it, picks up his mug, and reads the inscription on the picture*) Till death us do part.

There is a very loud crash of thunder right overhead. The lights flicker and go out, leaving the room once more lit only by firelight. Sam glances upwards, then down at the picture again. He lifts his mug in a toast (*Loudly*) Here's to you, Alice—wherever you are. (*He drinks*)

The door L *opens wide to reveal Alice in a flowing gown standing in the doorway. She slides into the room*

Alice (*softly but firmly*) I'm right behind you.

Sam chokes, the cocoa sprays out in a fountain as he spins round to see her

Surprised?

Sam (*weakly*) Alice . . . (*He gives another choking cough, and his mouth opens and closes silently*)

Alice Gone quiet, haven't you?

Sam tries to speak, but is unable to

What's wrong? Cat got your tongue?

He shakes his head weakly

You've had plenty to say about me these last few days, haven't you? Why run dry now?

Sam (*shaking his head to clear it*) It's the drink. I've had too much to drink.

Alice I'll say you have. Look at you. You look like a second-hand scarecrow and your breath smells like a brewery's bottling department. Sam Early, I could *murder* you.

Sam (*his eyes wide*) You're dead.

Alice Of course I'm dead, you big drunken half-wit. Why do you think I'm dressed like this, eh? For Hallowe'en?

Sam I knew I shouldn't have had that last pint. (*He sits on the sofa*)

Alice (*firmly*) Don't sit down when I'm talking to you!

Sam jumps up quickly

Sam (*realizing with dawning horror*) It *is* you.

Alice Well it's certainly not Mabel Sutton come back to flaunt her best bit of Marks and Sparks flanelette at you.

Sam's mouth opens

Yes—she saw me, all right—and I saw her. (*Fiercely*) What was she doing round here in her night clothes, eh?

Sam (*startled*) Nothing.

Alice Just paying a social visit, like? Is that all?

Sam Well . . .

Alice At quarter to one at night? (*Murderously*) Sam Early—if there's anything going on between you and Mabel Sutton, I'll . . .

Sam (*protesting*) There isn't. (*Annoyed*) Don't talk daft, woman. How could there be with Joe here as well?

Alice You could have been holding an orgy, for all I know.

Sam (*incredulously*) With Mabel Sutton?

Alice And why not? I know what you men are like when you've got a skinful of ale inside you. No better than animals. Oh, yes. My mother warned me about what drink did to a man. Warned me years ago.

Before I even married you. (*She points to the empty beer bottle by the sofa where Mabel left it*) And what's *that*?

Sam (*looking*) What?

Alice *That!* Beer bottles in my house.

Sam *Your* house??

Alice Yes—MY house! I might be dead, Sam Early, but I'm not gone yet. Not by a long chalk, I'm not. And I'll let you into a little secret, shall I? I'm *not* going.

Sam (*startled*) You mean—you're thinking of stopping?

Alice I'm not thinking of it at all. I've thought. So you'd better get used to the idea of having me around the place again, because it looks as if I'm going to be here for quite a long time.

Sam But—but you *can't*. You can't stop. What about the neighbours?

Alice You needn't worry. I've seen 'em all before, so I won't be frightened by 'em.

Sam But what if *they* see *you*?

Alice They won't. I'm reserving that pleasure for you alone—unless you try to slip a fast one on me—and in that case—you'll just have to watch out for fireworks.

Sam Well—won't they miss you from up there.

Alice (*stiffening*) No—because I'm not from up there.

Sam (*startled*) You mean . . . (*He glances down at the floor*)

Alice (*tartly*) And I'm not from down there, either. I'm from nowhere. I refused to go anywhere until I'd been allowed to come back here and sort some unfinished business out.

Sam Refused? You mean—they gave you a choice?

Alice Of course they didn't give me a choice. *I* gave *them* one. Either I came back here to do what I wanted to, or they suffered the consequences. It didn't take 'em long to decide which one it were going to be.

Sam (*nodding*) I can imagine.

Alice Yes—I'm sure you can.

Sam Anyway—what sort of thing is it you want to settle back here? If it's about that second-hand coffin . . .

Alice It's not. Sit down.

Sam I'd rather stand, if you don't mind.

Alice (*firmly*) Sit.

Sam sits quickly on the sofa

Now then . . . Just keep your mouth closed and listen to what I'm going to tell you. (*She moves down to him*) In the first place—this house is an absolute pighole. It were never like this when I were alive, and it's not going to be like this now I've come back. First thing tomorrow morning you're going to give it a good going over from top to bottom. Understand? There's nobody going to look down their noses at *my* family. In the second place—you're going to learn to cook.

Sam Eh?

Alice You heard. By the look of that kitchen you've lived on nothing but tinned beans, frozen peas and fish and chips for the last week.

Sam Well . . .

Alice Well nothing. Frozen food's too expensive for a start. Good fresh veg is what I gave you, and that's what you're going to keep getting. I'll work out a menu for the week, and we can go through it step by step. You'll do it and I'll watch. You'll soon learn. Our Terry'll be going back to his job on Monday, I take it, and he's not going to do a good day's work on a bellyful of toast and coffee—neither are you.

Sam Why should you care what we eat?

Alice Because I'm your wife—and his mother.

Sam But you're dead, Alice. You've got no right to come back here.

Alice Who says I haven't? I've not looked after you two all these years just to watch you go to pieces the minute I'm out the way. Oh, no. "Start as you mean to go on" is my motto.

Sam But you've *finished*!

Alice Not yet, I haven't—because now I'm coming to point number three.

Sam And what's that?

Alice Our Terry.

Sam What about him?

Alice He's not to marry that girl.

Sam Eh?

Alice I want that engagement breaking off, and I want it done fast . . . before things get out of hand. You've *got* to talk to him.

Sam I can't.

Alice Why not? You're his father. He might listen to you.

Sam Well he'll have to listen a long time then, Alice, because I'm having nothing to do with it.

Alice Oh yes you are, Sam Early. He is not going to marry that girl and that's final.

Sam Just you try and stop him.

Alice (*quietly*) And do you think I can't?

Sam looks at her doubtfully

We've got some strange powers, us that have passed over. I could make things rather hot for him—and you.

Sam (*with doubtful bravado*) Huh.

Alice You wouldn't like to see him get—hurt—would you, Sam?

Sam Hurt?

Alice That's what I said.

Sam But—he's your own lad.

Alice And yours, Sam. And yours.

Sam looks down

I'll give you twenty-four hours to see that he gets that ring back. All right?

Sam (*after a pause*) How?

Alice That's your problem, Sam—not mine. Where is he?

Sam (*miserably*) He's taking Susan back to Hightown.

Alice No matter. It'll be for the last time, won't it, Sam?

Sam is silent

I said, won't it?

Sam (*quietly*) I suppose so.

Alice (*smiling*) Well that's all right then, isn't it? We can all settle down again just as if nothing had happened. And just to show there's no ill feelings, I'll go do all the washing-up for you. (*She moves towards the door* R)

Sam (*suddenly*) Just a minute, Alice.

Alice (*turning*) Yes?

Sam You—er—you did say earlier on that—well—that there'd only be *me* who could see you, didn't you?

Alice Unless you step out of line, yes.

Sam So if I don't do as you tell me to—you're going to show yourself to somebody else, are you?

Alice I'll show meself to half the neighbourhood if needs be, but I don't think there'll be any call for that to happen, because you're *going* to do just as I tell you to do, the way you always *did* do and the way you're going to *keep on* doing. Is that quite clear?

Sam No—I'm afraid it isn't, Alice. You see—you still haven't explained why I'm the only one you want to see you.

Alice I'd have thought that that would have been obvious. It's because I'd object very much to being pointed at and examined as though I were some kind of freak.

Sam But you are, Alice. You are.

Alice reacts

You see, you're dead—a ghost. And ghosts are something strange to a lot of folks. You're summat millions of people don't believe in, yet here you are—roaming around my house.

Alice *My* house, if you don't mind.

Sam No, Alice. Mine. This is my house—and you're my ghost. I'm going to make a fortune out of you.

Alice You're *what*?

Sam That's right. I'm going to make millions. I'll charge ten pence a head to look at you. Sell photos. Everything. They'll come from all over the world.

Alice (*grimly*) Oh, no they won't. Not into this house, they won't.

Sam (*chortling*) But they will, Alice, they will. It'll be a bigger attraction than Blackpool Tower.

Alice (*furiously*) You let one person through that front door, Sam Early, and I'll—I'll . . .

Sam What? Start throwing things? (*He rubs his hands*) Even better. I could charge more for that. I'd have a notice hung up outside saying "Come in and see the real flying saucers" and you could make a start with that awful tea service your Doris gave us for a wedding present.

Alice Sam . . .

Sam (*excitedly*) And follow it up with that lop-sided vase your Ethel palmed us off with when she came back from Clacton.

Alice Sam . . .

Sam (*chortling*) I can hear the turnstiles clicking and the tills tinkling right now.

Alice Well in that case, you want to get your ears seen to as soon as possible. If you think you're going to put me on exhibition, Sam Early, you've got another think coming. I'm not going to be gawped at by a load of mindless morons who've got nothing better to do with their time and money. Not under any circumstances I'm not.

Sam You've no choice, Alice. Because I'm certainly not going to toe the line, as you call it, and there isn't a thing you can do to make me do it.

Alice Isn't there? (*She scowls*)

Sam No, there isn't. You appear to anybody else but me, and the coach parties move in within twenty-four hours. Understand?

Alice (*grimly*) All right. You've asked for it. From this moment on you're going to be the only one who'll set eyes on me until that engagement's broken off.

Sam Well in that case, you can stop here and haunt me till you're black in the face, because I'm not going to lift a finger to break off our Terry's engagement, and that's final.

Alice What did you say?

Sam You heard. She's a grand lass is young Susan, and if our Terry wants to marry her, then he's going to, and there's neither you nor anybody else going to stop him.

Alice Have you taken leave of your senses?

Sam I don't think so, Alice. I'm just letting you realize that you don't run things around here any more. You can't order me about like you used to. Not any more, you can't. You're dead, you see—like it or lump it—and from now on, I'm the one who gives the orders here.

Alice You? (*She laughs*) Now just you listen to me, Sam Early——

Sam (*loudly*) No! You listen to me for a change. I spent nineteen years of my life listening to you, and that's enough for any man. Our Terry's going to marry that girl, and there's nothing you can say or do about it.

Alice (*breathing heavily*) Isn't there?

Sam No, there isn't. And don't think you can scare me with that threat about doing something to him—because if you harm one hair of his head—I'll fill this place with tourists so fast they'll have the shroud off your back before you can say Jack Robinson. (*He gulps*)

Alice (*after a pause*) I see. So you're going to defy me, are you?

Sam Yes. (*He sits on the sofa*)

Alice Stand up!

Sam jumps up quickly

We'll see about that. You've just made a bad mistake, Sam, a very bad mistake.

Sam I made my biggest mistake nineteen years ago when I married you on the rebound from Reuben Rickworth.

Alice Sam . . .

Sam If you want to try and stop our Terry getting wed, then you'd better get cracking on it yourself—but I'll warn you, Alice. I'll fight you every inch of the way.

Alice But you don't understand . . .⁓

Sam Oh yes I do. You want me to settle a grudge for you by spoiling that lass's life the way you spoiled mine.

Alice Spoiled . . .?

Sam Aye—spoiled. That's what I said.

Alice (*tightening her lips*) So that's the way it's going to be, is it?

Sam It is.

Alice Right. (*She opens the door* R) Then you'll have to face the consequences for what's going to happen.

Sam Where are you going?

Alice Back to—where I came from.

Sam Oh. So you realize you're beaten then, do you?

Alice Beaten? (*She smiles sweetly*) Sam, love—I haven't even started yet.

Alice exits quickly R

Sam Alice! (*He dashes o the door* R) Alice—wait!

Sam exits R

(*Off*) Alice—just a minute . . .!

Sam enters L

Alice? (*He looks round*) She's gone. (*He shakes his head to clear it*) I—I must have been dreaming. Aye—that's it—I've had a drop too much and started seeing things. (*He sits on the sofa*) It seemed that real, too.

The lights flicker and come back on

(*He laughs and sighs*) Well—I certainly don't mind *you* coming back. (*He shakes his head*) Of all the things to see, though. Alice . . . (*He runs his hand through his hair*) Why couldn't I see pink elephants, same as everybody else? (*He laughs*) By heck! If only I could have spoken to her like that when she were still alive. Things might have been a lot different. (*He rises*) It seemed that *real*, though. I could have sworn . . . (*He sighs*) Talk about the mind playing tricks. I'd best get off to bed. Try to sleep it off. (*He moves towards the door* L)

Terry enters L. *He wears his jacket*

Terry (*as he enters*) It's stopped raining. (*He sees Sam*) What's up, Dad? You look as though you've seen a ghost.

Sam Aye. Aye—well I'm just a bit tired, lad. Must get some sleep. It's been a bit of a rough week what with one thing and another.

Terry (*removing his jacket*) Yes. (*Pause*) Dad . . .?

Sam (*at the door*) Aye?

Terry It is all right, isn't it? I mean . . . you don't mind? About me and Susan. (*He hangs his coat on a chair back*)

Sam (*smiling*) Course it's all right. Why should I mind?

Terry Well . . . (*He moves down to the sofa*) It's just that—thinking about that last day—when Mum died . . .

Sam Now look, lad—don't you start getting a guilty conscience.

Terry (*sitting*) No—it's not that—it's just that—well—we've been talking things over—me and Susan—and we wondered—well—if you thought we should have waited—before we got engaged.

Sam (*coming back*) Look . . .

Terry I mean—I suppose it does look bad—getting engaged the week after your own mother dies . . .

Sam Terry . . .

Terry (*looking up at Sam*) If only she hadn't been so *against* Susan—I wouldn't have done it—you know—announced it so soon.

Sam (*gently*) Look, lad—it wouldn't have made any difference *when* you did it. Not to me. All I want is for you to be happy. That's all. (*He puts his hand on Terry's shoulder*)

Terry (*taking hold of Sam's hand momentarily*) Thank's, Dad. (*He rises*) We *are* in love. Honest, we are.

Sam I'm sure you are. (*He grins*) Eh, you youngsters are all the same. You think love's some kind of beautiful dream.

Terry (*smiling*) And isn't it?

Sam Oh, aye—but marriage is a dratted alarm clock.

Terry It can't be all that bad, Dad. Look at old Mrs Penkirk. She's been married five times.

Sam Yes . . . and look what happened the last time she walked down the aisle. Instead of playing the *Wedding March*, the organist played *Here we are again.*

They both laugh

Terry (*seriously*) You don't think we're too young, though?

Sam You'll always be too young if you listen to your parents, lad. They don't want to lose you, you see. But you go on. Spread your wings and the best of luck to you both.

Terry (*relieved*) Like they say—you're only on this earth once, aren't you?

Sam (*cautiously*) Er—yes. I think.

Terry You don't sound too sure about it.

Sam Aye—well it's best not to be too sure of anything, these days.

Terry Oh, I don't know. I mean—*I'm* sure I want to marry Susan—and somehow, I feel sure that if Mum were still alive she'd have changed her mind and let us go ahead without any more fuss. I mean—she can't have had any real grudge against her, can she?

Sam No—no—course she couldn't.

Terry It was just that thing with Mr Rickworth, wasn't it?

The door R *opens quickly and quietly to admit Alice. The door closes behind her*

Sam's eyes pop

Alice (*to Sam*) What was that? What did he say?
Terry It was all so stupid. Holding a grudge all those years. Don't *you* think so, Dad?
Alice (*to Sam*) Have you *told* him?
Sam (*gulping*) Yes—I mean—no.
Terry (*surprised*) No? Why not?
Alice Then who did?
Sam Mind your own business.
Terry Sorry. I didn't know you felt . . .
Sam (*quickly*) No—no. Not you, lad. I wasn't talking to you.
Terry (*surprised*) Not talking . . .? (*He looks around, puzzled*)
Alice What does he know about the Rickworths? Answer me!
Sam Terry—look. Over there. (*He points to Alice*)

Terry looks at Alice and back to Sam

Can you see—anything?
Alice Of course he can't, you fathead.
Terry Like what?
Sam Anything.
Terry (*baffled*) The door?
Alice I told you.
Sam (*to Terry*) Nip down to Joe's and tell him I'd like him to come back here—quick as he can.
Terry Mr Gittings? But Dad—it's nearly two in the morning.
Alice (*to Sam*) And what do you think *he's* going to do for you?
Sam (*to Terry*) Quick. Kick his door down if you have to, but get him.

Terry gives a puzzled look at Sam, then quickly exits past Alice through the door R

Alice I asked you what he knew about the Rickworths. What have you told him?
Sam What do you think I've told him? I've told him everything.
Alice Then—he knows?
Sam Of course he knows. He'd a right to. Every right.
Alice (*shaking her head*) Oh, Sam—Sam.
Sam And it's no use you standing there saying "Sam, Sam". That's not going to change anything.
Alice (*fiercely*) You *fool*!
Sam Eh?
Alice I warned you, didn't I? I *warned* you.
Sam (*baffled*) What about?

Alice Now you've *really* gone and let the cat out of the bag.

Sam What cat? Why try to keep it a secret? You were jilted, Alice, that's all. You weren't the first one it ever happened to, and you won't be the last, so what's all the fuss about?

Alice I—I can't tell you, Sam.

Sam (*puzzled*) Why not?

Alice Because—because I *can't*. That's why. You've upset everything. I was going to risk it—but now—well, it's no use. You've got to stop him before it's too late.

Sam I'm stopping nobody.

Alice (*loudly*) Then *I* will!

Terry enters breathlessly R

Terry He's coming. Just getting a coat. I had to knock him up. What's wrong?

Sam Nothing, lad. Not a thing.

Alice (*to Sam*) For the last time . . .

Sam (*loudly*) No!

Terry (*bewildered*) Dad?

Sam Listen, Terry—there's something I'm going to tell you . . .

Alice Sam. No . . .

Sam (*ignoring her*) It's your mother. She's come back to haunt us.

Terry (*baffled*) Eh?

Sam She's standing right over there—by the door. Watching us.

Terry (*concerned*) Are you O.K., Dad?

Sam *louder*) Of course I'm O.K. She's there, I tell you. I can see her.

Terry Look—Dad—hadn't you better sit down for a few minutes? Mr Gittings'll be here soon. (*He touches Sam's shoulder timidly*)

Sam No. No—I want to keep an eye on her—see she doesn't vanish again like last time. (*He pushes Terry's hand away*)

Alice Sam . . .

Terry (*worried*) Take it easy, Dad . . .

Sam She wants me to make you break off the engagement, but I'm not going to do it. (*To Alice*) I'm not going to do it. Do you hear?

Terry Dad . . .

The door R *opens and Mabel Sutton appears in the opening*

Mabel (*looking straight through Alice*) Is something the matter?

Sam Mabel . . .

Mabel I saw your Terry go dashing round to Joe Gittings's, so I thought there must be something wrong.

Alice (*turning to glower*) Nosey old cat.

Terry It's me dad . . .

Sam It's *not*. It's her. (*He points at Alice*)

Mabel (*surprised*) Me? And what have I done now?

Sam Nothing. It's Alice. Standing right in front of you.

Mabel stares at Alice, then at Terry

Mabel He's gone crackers. Off his rocker. (*She backs against the door in horror*)

Sam (*howling*) But you saw her too. Outside—in the street.

Mabel (*to Terry*) That were just a sheet of polythene in the wind. Joe Gittings brought it in here to show me.

Sam It *wasn't*. It was all a mistake. It was Alice. *Alice*. ALICE!

The door R *opens again, throwing Mabel forward on to the sofa back. Joe Gittings rushes in wearing a long flannel nightgown with a coat over the top. His big working boots, and his flat cap*

Joe (*entering*) What's to do? What's up?

Mabel rubs her bottom. Alice moves to the end of the sofa

Sam Joe . . . (*He rushes to him*) We made a mistake. It *was* Alice, Mabel saw out there. She's here. In this room, standing right there. (*He indicates the end of the sofa*) By the end of the sofa.

Joe (*seizing on the implications*) Oh—aye—aye—so she is, Sam. Right at the end of the sofa. (*Aside to Mabel*) Go phone for the doctor. (*He turns back and gets hold of Sam's shoulders*)

Mabel (*glancing at Sam*) 'Sylum's more like it.

Alice (*to Sam*) Now look what you've done, you great booby. They think you want locking up.

Sam (*startled*) Eh? No—no—I don't. There's nothing wrong with me. She's there, Joe. Right there. (*He tries to turn but Joe holds on*)

Mabel scurries round the front of the sofa to Terry

Mabel You'd better come with me to the phone, Terry. You've got your clothes on. (*She grabs Terry's arm*)

Sam Wait. (*He spins round to face them as Joes hold relaxes*) Terry—help me.

Joe (*tightening his hold*) Don't worry, Sam. We'll help you, all right. It's just strain, that's all. Just strain. (*To Mabel*) Hurry up.

Mabel (*to Terry*) Come on.

Sam No. (*To Alice*) It's all your fault. (*He breaks free of Joe and rushes at Alice, arms outstretched for her shoulders*) Yours!

Alice moves slightly and Sam "passes through" her heading straight for Mabel who is in direct line. Mabel screams with fright as he grabs her and passes out in a dead faint in Terry's arms. Joe rushes after Sam and pulls him away

Terry ⎱ Dad . . .
Joe ⎰ Sam . . .
Sam ⎰ Alice . . . ⎱ (*Speaking together*)
Alice ⎰ Sam . . . ⎰

Sam (*struggling*) Let go of me. Let go.

Joe (*holding on*) Steady on, Sam—steady on. Terry . . .

Terry lowers Mabel to the floor quickly

Terry Hold on a minute.

  Terry dashes out of the door L

Alice (*to Sam*) Stop it, you fool . . .
Sam (*wildly*) Let go of me. Let go. Let gooooooooooo.

They stagger backwards to the sofa

Joe Give over, Sam. Give over.

  Terry rushes back in holding a large copper warming-pan

Terry Look out, Mr Gittings. Look out. (*He swings the pan above his head*)
Alice No . . . (*She closes her eyes*)
Joe (*moving aside quickly and releasing Sam*) Now . . .!

Terry swings the pan as Sam turns. Too late he sees it coming. The pan connects. Sam's head goes right through the bottom of it, and emerges through the lid. He stands there, eyes glazed, then slowly crumples on to the sofa unconscious still wearing it like a collar. Joe and Terry look down at him, then at each other. Alice shakes her head slowly as—

the CURTAIN *falls*

ACT II

Scene 1

The same. One week later, Sunday afternoon

When the CURTAIN *rises, the room is neat and tidy. A white cloth is on the table, and cups, saucers, plates and cutlery are in position. A plate of iced buns on the table. Milk bottle and sugar bowl are by the upstage chair.*

The curtains are open and the fire is lit

Joe is sitting on the sofa in his usual trouser and sweater, etc., but this time has a once-decent tweed coat on. He holds a mug of tea. Sam is pacing backwards and forwards behind him, wearing a worried look. He wears almost the same clothing as in the previous scene, but this time a clean shirt, open at the neck and no cardigan

Joe (*after a few moments*) For goodness sake, Sam. Sit down, can't you? You're giving me the willies.

Sam (*distraught*) Giving *you* the willies? How do you think *I* feel?

Joe Well, wearing a path out in the carpet won't help matters, will it? Now park your backside and calm down.

Sam (*leaning over the sofa back*) How can I calm down when I don't know what *she's* up to?

Joe Who?

Sam Who do you think? Alice, of course. (*He straightens*)

Joe (*groaning*) Oh, we're not on *that* subject again, are we?

Sam What do you mean—again? We never left it so far as I'm concerned.

Joe (*wearily*) Sam, she's dead.

Sam I know she's dead. That's what's worrying me, isn't it? I paid to have her cremated, and I want to know what she's doing walking in and out of here as if she still ran the place. It's not decent.

Joe (*gently*) Look, Sam—are you sure you didn't *dream* it all? After all— we did stop some beer from going bad last Saturday, you know.

Sam (*exasperated*) Joe—for the last time—I did not dream it. I wasn't drunk. I wasn't off me rocker—and Alice was HERE! She wanted me to break off our Terry's engagement to young Susan Rickworth.

Joe Aye—so you keep saying.

Sam Then why don't you believe me? (*He moves restlessly to the table*) Oh, what's the use? It's like talking to a brick wall.

Joe All right—all right. Supposing I was to believe you. Then what? Suppose Alice *is* haunting you.

Sam (*turning to face him*) But she *isn't*. That's the whole flaming trouble.

Joe (*baffled*) But you've just said . . .

Sam (*flinging his hands in the air*) You see? You weren't even *listening* to me, were you? I've just told you. She *was* haunting me—but now she *isn't*—and I don't know which is worst.

Joe Well if she's not haunting you now—what's all the fuss about?

Sam (*moving over to the sofa*) Because I don't know what she's *doing*. That's what it's all about. (*He sits on the sofa arm*)

Joe Happen she's gone back to where she came from, then? You know— to rest in peace.

Sam Rest in peace? Alice? Don't make me laugh. If I know her, she's floating around somewhere cooking up something that's going to make the Spanish Inquisition sound like nursery school. If you hadn't inter- fered last week, I could have had all this lot settled by now.

Joe If I hadn't interfered last week, you might have been sitting in Castle- ford Police Station on a strangulation charge. Poor old Mabel couldn't speak for two days with the shock of it. Besides—it weren't me what hit you with that warming-pan—it were your Terry.

Sam (*gingerly touching his head as he rises*) Don't remind me about that. I've still got the lump.

Joe How's it feeling?

Sam I'll live. Anyway, never mind about my head—I was on about Alice, wasn't I? Like I was saying—when I came round again—she'd gone— and I've not seen hair nor hide of her since. I'm telling you straight, Joe— she's got me worried.

Joe Ah, cheer up, Sam. P'raps she's given it up as a bad job, eh?

Sam (*shaking his head*) Not her. No—she's just waiting her chance to split 'em up once and for all—and if that isn't enough for me to worry about—there's our Terry. He hasn't been able to look me in the eye all week.

Joe He'll come round before long. I told him it were just the strain you'd been under what caused it.

Sam Strain he says.

Joe Well, I had to tell him something, didn't I—and Mabel. Another two minutes and you'd have had the little men in white coats coming round to collect you.

Sam Aye, and if I don't find out what *she's* up to in the next few hours, they might still be coming. (*He runs his hand through his hair*) Oh, Joe— I'm going crackers—I know I am.

Joe Course you're not. You're just letting things get you down a bit, that's all.

Sam (*helplessly*) Do you think so, Joe? Honestly?

Joe Course I do. It's only natural isn't it? You don't get over a shock like your wife dying sudden in a few days, you know. It's hard to lose a wife.

Sam Hard? It's damned impossible.

Joe Never mind, Sam. Soon as you've got this afternoon off your chest you'll be as right as rain. After all—this'll be an extra strain on you an' all, won't it? Meeting your son's prospective in-laws for the first time.

Sam Well, hardly for the first time. I were at school with Reuben.

Joe Aye, well you know what I mean. It's the first time in your own home, isn't it? They've not been down here before?

Sam Never. Alice wouldn't have let 'em come within shouting distance let alone set foot in the place.

Joe There you are, then. What time are they arriving?

Sam Any time now.

Joe In that case I'd better be off. (*He finishes his tea off and rises*)

Sam Nay—don't go, Joe. Sit yourself down. I'll need a bit of moral support. You know what I'm like at meeting folks.

Joe Well—if you're sure.

Sam Aye—aye. Have another cup of tea. (*He takes hold of Joe's mug*)

Mabel (*off* R) Anybody in?

Sam (*calling*) NO!

Joe reseats himself on the sofa

Mabel enters R

Mabel Hello, Sam—feeling better, are you? I just thought I'd pop round and see how you . . . (*She spots the set table*) Oh. Expecting company, I see.

Sam Aye. (*He moves to the table to pour more tea for Joe*)

Mabel (*sweetly*) Anybody I know?

Sam Probably. (*He picks up the teapot*)

Mabel (*persisting*) Friends, like?

Sam (*pouring*) No, I wouldn't call 'em friends exactly.

Mabel Oh. Just "somebody special", like?

Sam That's right, Mabel.

Mabel I thought it must be. (*She beams at Sam and Joe*)

Sam Did you? (*He adds milk*)

Mabel I could *tell*, you see.

Sam Could you? (*He moves back to Joe with the tea*)

Mabel (*moving closer to the table*) Because of the tea things.

Sam Oh?

Mabel (*trying to be bright*) It were Alice's best one, you see.

Sam Were it?

Mabel (*knowingly*) Oh, yes. She only got that set out when she had somebody special in to tea.

Joe I bet she never had it out for you.

Mabel (*sniffing at Joe's remark*) So that's how I guessed, you see. Because of the tea service.

Sam Aye—well you guessed wrong then, didn't you? 'Cos it just happened to be the first one I came across in the cupboard.

Mabel Oh, I don't think Alice'd be very pleased about you doing that.

Joe That's all right, Mabel—she's not been invited.

Mabel (*to Sam*) Do you work him with your foot? (*To Joe*) I suppose you'll be having your great plates of meat under the table, though, won't you? You'll not miss the chance of a free meal.

Joe (*cheerfully*) Not if I can help it, Mabel.

Mabel Well you needn't bother yourself coming round to our house for anything, Joe Gittings, 'cos you'll get nothing from *me*.

Joe That's all right, Mabel. I'm none so fond of salads, anyway.

Mabel (*taken aback*) Who said owt about salads?

Joe Nobody. Only I know you're having salad today, 'cos I saw you over the road this morning, pulling up dandelions.

Mabel Oh, very funny—I don't think. You ought to be on the stage, you did. *Scrubbing* it!

Sam (*moving back to the table*) Oh, knock it off, you two. They'll be here in a minute.

Mabel (*quickly*) Who will?

Sam (*smiling*) The company.

Mabel (*defeated*) Oh . . . Well—I suppose I'd better be going then—unless you'd like me to stop and give a hand, eh?

Sam just looks at her silently

'Course, I wouldn't like to intrude if it's going to be something—private.

Joe Wouldn't you?

Mabel (*snapping at him*) No, I wouldn't. I'm not like *some* folks I could mention. I believe in keeping my nose out of things what don't concern me.

Joe Aye, you might believe it, but it doesn't mean you *do* it.

Mabel Are you insinuating I'm nosey, Joe Gittings?

Joe Nosey? You've got a longer nose than Pinocchio.

Mabel (*stung*) Oh.

Sam (*tiredly*) Steady on, Joe. (*He sits at the table*)

Mabel I should think so as well. I'm not the least bit interested in other folks' business. Like I've always said—if you can't invite folks round to your own home without having to tell the whole neighbourhood about it, it's a bit of a bad job.

Joe Here, here.

Mabel nods indignantly then turns to Sam

Mabel So what time are you expecting them, Sam? These friends of yours?

Sam I've told you. Any time now.

Mabel You'll be able to see them coming down the front street then, won't you? That is, always assuming they'll come down the front street, eh?

Sam They will.

Mabel I'd better get off then. (*She smiles at them both, and backs to the door* R)

Joe You should just have time to position yourself behind the curtains.

Mabel glares at him

Oh—and don't forget a glass of water.

Mabel What for? (*She moves back behind Joe*)

Joe It'll stop the dust getting in your throat.

Mabel (*frostily*) I shall ignore that remark, Joe Gittings. Them curtains of mine get washed almost as often as—as . . . (*She tries to think of something*)

Joe For goodness sake don't say your Eustace. He's not had a wash since the midwife did it.

Mabel (*to Sam*) If there's anything *you* want to borrow at any time, Sam—especially if your—friends are here—you've only to knock on the wall. (*She marches angrily to the door* R)

Sam That's all right, Mabel. I wouldn't want to bother you.

Mabel (*in the doorway, sweetly*) It'll be no bother, Sam. After all—any friend of yours is a friend of mine.

Joe That's wishful thinking.

There is a knocking at the front door off L

Mabel (*pleased*) Oh—that'll be them. I'll go let 'em in, shall I? (*She quickly runs her hands down her clothes*)

Sam (*quickly*) I'll do it. (*He hops rapidly to the door* L) You can go out the back way, can't you, Mabel?

Sam exits L

Mabel (*protesting*) But . . .

Joe (*moving round to her*) You heard. Out. (*He pushes her back into the doorway* R)

Sam (*off*) Hello. Come in, both of you. I'll take your coats.

Mabel (*struggling*) Take your hands off me.

Reuben (*off*) Not too early, are we, Sam?

Sam (*off*) Course not. It's through there.

Joe Out you go.

Joe pushes Mabel out and closes the door R. *The door* L *opens and Reuben Rickworth enters, followed by Lucy Rickworth and Sam. Reuben is about the same age as Sam, but a little more burly. He is dressed in a dark suit a little too tight for him, and looks rather uncomfortable. Lucy is a small woman of nearly forty, dressed in a flowery frock, white gloves, shoes, and carrying a white handbag. The effect is rather sad*

Reuben (*nodding to Joe*) How do.

Joe 'Lo.

Lucy (*timidly*) Hello.

Joe (*nodding*) 'Lo.

Sam (*indicating*) Joe Gittings—Mr and Mrs Rickworth.

Joe (*nodding*) Hello.

Reuben 'Lo.

Lucy Hello.

There is a silence. All stand looking at one another

Sam (*suddenly*) Wouldn't you like to sit down?
Joe Oh—thanks. (*He moves round to sit on the sofa*)

Lucy and Reuben look at each other then sit. Reuben next to Joe, Lucy at the middle chair by the table

Sam (*still standing, to Lucy*) You're quite sure you're comfortable there, Mrs Rickworth?
Lucy (*shyly*) Yes, thank you.
Sam You can sit on the sofa, if you'd like?
Lucy (*coyly*) No thank you.
Reuben (*standing*) Course you would. Come on, love. Have this.
Lucy (*simpering*) All right, then. (*She stands and goes to sit beside Joe*)
Reuben There. That's better. (*He sits on the chair*)

Lucy and Joe smile at each other

Sam All comfy now, then?
Lucy (*smiling*) Yes, thank you.
Reuben Aye. Aye. I'm all right.

There is another silence

Joe (*suddenly*) Would you like to sit here, Reuben, lad—by your missis? (*He rises*)
Reuben No. No—it's all right—er—Joe. You stay where you are.
Joe No—no—you come and sit by Mrs Rickworth. (*He moves to the table*)
Lucy You *can* call me Lucy. (*She simpers*)
Reuben Well, all right, then. (*He rises and moves back to the sofa to sit next to Lucy*)
Joe There. (*He sits in the chair*)
Sam (*coughing nervously*) All settled again?
Reuben Yes thank you.
Joe Oh, aye. All settled. (*He smiles at Reuben and Lucy*)
Sam Well then . . . (*He stops and looks lost*)

There is an awkward pause

Reuben (*looking round*) Nice room.
Lucy Very.
Sam Oh? (*He smiles weakly*)
Reuben Nice house, in fact.
Lucy (*nodding*) Very nice.
Sam (*shrugging*) Not bad.
Joe (*shaking his head*) No.
Lucy (*leaning forward*) Pardon?
Joe I said "no". It isn't.
Sam (*blinking*) What isn't?
Joe (*indicating*) This. It isn't bad.

Sam What?
Reuben The house.
Lucy It's not bad.
Sam Oh. No. No—it's not.

There is another silence. Sam looks at Joe in a pleading manner

Joe (*suddenly*) Would you like a cup of tea?
Lucy (*brightening*) Well, we wouldn't say no, though we did have one before we came out, didn't we, Reuben?
Reuben Aye.
Sam I'll go make a pot, then, shall I?
Joe (*rising*) No—I'll do it, Sam. You stop and entertain Mr and Mrs . . . (*He indicates Reuben and Lucy*)
Sam Oh. Yes—well all right, then.
Lucy It wouldn't be too much trouble to ask for lemon with mine, would it, Mr Gittings?
Joe Lemon?
Sam Instead of milk, she means.
Joe Oh. Well, have you got one?
Sam (*shaking his head*) No.
Lucy Oh. Well—it doesn't matter. Not really.
Reuben She will take milk, won't you, love?
Lucy Of course I will—if you haven't got lemon. Yes.
Sam I haven't.
Lucy Well it doesn't matter then, does it? (*She smiles*)
Sam I can go out and get one.
Joe On Sunday?
Sam Oh.
Reuben She can do without, Sam. It doesn't have to be lemon.
Lucy No, it doesn't matter. I'll have milk. It's just that I prefer lemon, that's all.
Sam I'm sorry. I didn't know.
Lucy No—of course you didn't. Or else you'd have had one in, wouldn't you?
Sam Aye.

The door R opens and Mabel sidles in

Mabel (*sweetly*) Sorry to butt in when you've got company, Sam, but I thought you might like one of these. (*She holds up a lemon*) So useful, lemons are. I use them all the time. (*She beams at the Rickworths to get a good look at them*) YOU! (*She drops the lemon in shock*)
Reuben Hello, Mabel.
Lucy (*quietly but firmly*) Hello.
Mabel (*taken aback*) Well, I must say—you're the last people I ever expected to see in *this* house . . .
Sam (*warningly*) Mabel . . .
Mabel Not that *I* could ever see what Alice Early had against you. I

mean. It's far better to make a clean break before the wedding than to try to do it afterwards, wouldn't you say? Marry in haste repent in leisure I believe the term is—not that *you've* had to repent, of course.

Reuben No—we haven't.

Lucy (*cuttingly*) And we didn't marry in haste, either.

Mabel No—no. Of course not. I never *did* believe *that* tale.

Sam Well thanks for the lemon, Mabel. I'll see you get one back for it, later. (*He picks up the lemon from where it fell*)

Mabel Oh, it doesn't matter. I never have any use for 'em. Too bitter.

Joe (*lifting the teapot*) I'll go put that kettle on.

Joe exits R

Mabel (*to Lucy*) You—er—you haven't altered much, Lucy.

Lucy (*pointedly*) Neither have you.

Mabel (*simpering*) Oh, I don't know. My waistline's got a bit bigger. (*She smooths her waist, then perches on the sofa arm*)

Sam (*aside, with venom*) And your mouth.

Mabel (*reminiscing*) It's been a few years, hasn't it?

Lucy (*shortly*) Yes.

Mabel I have been meaning to come up to the shop and have a chat with you, but I never seem to get a free minute.

Reuben I know. You can't cram much into nineteen years, can you?

Lucy Reuben.

Mabel Well—you know how things are, don't you?

Lucy I know how they *were*.

Mabel (*uneasy*) Yes . . . (*She looks over her shoulder*) He—he won't be long with that tea.

Sam Aye—well I'll let you know if there's anything else we need, Mabel.

Mabel (*brightly*) Yes, of course. Just say the word and I can pop round and get it. (*To Lucy*) That's always supposing I've got it, isn't it? (*She gives a false laugh*)

Lucy Aren't *you* going to sit down, Mr Early?

Mabel Oh, call him Sam. Everybody else does. No need to stand on ceremony here, you know.

Sam I'm all right, thanks. I'll just see Mabel out.

Mabel (*with another false laugh*) Anybody'd think he were trying to get rid of me.

Sam I am.

Mabel (*startled*) I beg your pardon?

Reuben He said he was.

Mabel (*standing quickly and fuming*) What's the matter with me? Have I got the plague, or something?

Sam Mabel . . .

Mabel Don't you "Mabel" me, Sam Early. I can take a hint as good as the next one, I can. I know when I'm not wanted.

Reuben Well I should imagine you've had enough experience.

Lucy Reuben.

Mabel And you can keep your opinions to yourself, Reuben Rickworth. Think you're Mr High-and-Mighty you do, just because you own a run-down mucky tripe shop in Hightown. Well, I'll tell you this much for nothing—I wouldn't touch your tripe with a bargepole if I were starving.

Sam (*firmly*) Now that's enough.

Mabel (*ignoring him*) It were the best day's work you ever did, jilting poor Alice to run away wi' Lady Muck, there. Heaven knows what sort of life she'd have had with you, slaving away all hours that God sends, up to her elbows in stinking tripe.

Reuben (*stung*) Well that's better than living on State Charity like you do, Mabel Sutton. There's none of your lot done a decent day's work since they left school.

Mabel Don't you sneer at my kids, Reuben Rickworth. They're worth ten of you, they are. And anyway—what if they are on National Assistance? They're entitled to it. Our Eustace has a complaint.

Reuben Aye. Idle-itis.

Lucy Reuben.

Mabel You wouldn't dare talk like that to his face, would you? Oh, no. You only say things like that behind folks' backs. (*Fuming*) Oooh—I can't stand two-faced people.

Sam Hah!

Mabel (*snapping at him*) And you can keep your trap shut, Sam Early. There's nobody can accuse *me* of being two faced.

Sam That's true, Mabel. If you *were* two faced, you'd be better off wearing the other one.

Lucy Now, Sam . . .

Mabel (*glaring at Lucy*) And I don't need any help from *you*, either. I'm used to fighting me own battles.

Reuben Yes—but with the look of *your* face, you look like you've lost 'em all.

Joe enters R *with the teapot*

Joe Tea up.

Mabel (*turning on him*) And you can keep out of it, an' all.

Joe (*startled*) Eh? (*He looks at everybody in bewilderment*)

Sam I think you'd better go, Mabel.

Mabel I'll go when I'm good and ready. I'm going to have my say and nobody's going to stop me.

Joe (*moving to the table*) Oh, lor! Is she at it again?

Mabel Yes, she is at it again, and she'll stay at it till she gets an apology for what's just been said. I'm having nobody insult my family and getting away with it, so come on. Let's have it. Apologize. (*She folds her arms and glares at Reuben*)

Reuben You must be joking.

Mabel I shall stay here till you do.

Sam Oh, no you won't. We're going to have tea now, so you'd better be on your way.

Mabel You try and shift me.

Joe Stop acting like a fool, woman, and sling your hook.

Mabel Not till I get an apology.

Reuben You've got one. He's waiting for you at home.

Mabel (*incensed*) That's the *second* time I've been insulted here today.

Sam Aye, and you'll be insulted a third time, if you don't hurry up and shift yourself.

Mabel You wouldn't talk to me like that if your Alice were still alive. She'd have something to say about this lot, I can tell you. She'd have *plenty* to say.

Sam When didn't she have?

Lucy Now then, Samuel. You mustn't speak ill of the dead.

Mabel And you needn't come over all pious, Lucy Clayton. If it hadn't been for you fluttering your false eyelashes and waving your foam rubber at him there—(*indicating Reuben*)—she wouldn't have let herself be tricked into marriage with this thick-headed clod. (*She indicates Sam*)

Lucy I beg your pardon? (*She stands up grimly*)

Mabel (*sneering*) Don't come the innocent wi' *me*. You knew what you were doing all right. Stealing another woman's fiancé.

Reuben Nobody stole me. I went.

Mabel I never *did* reckon on anybody what married for money.

Lucy (*her eyes smouldering*) Would you mind repeating that last statement, Mrs Sutton?

Mabel Why? You've not gone deaf, have you? I said—some folks manage to find themself an husband without the chink of money having to guide 'em.

Lucy Yes—well we all know how you managed to catch *your* husband, don't we, Mrs Sutton?

Mabel Do we? And how *did* I manage to catch my husband, Mrs Rickworth?

Lucy Simple. He couldn't *run* fast enough.

Mabel (*astounded*) How dare you . . .?

Lucy (*with cold venom*) Quite easily—and I'll dare a lot more if you speak to me like that again, Mabel Sutton—or should I say—Holdsworth?

Mabel (*her jaw dropping*) Eh? (*She looks round in panic*) I don't know what you're talking about.

Lucy Don't you? Well *I* think you *do*. And if you open your foul mouth about us or our Susan again, there'll be a few more folks round here who'll be pricking their ears up—and that includes your precious little darlings the "Gruesome Twosome". Understand, Mrs—*Sutton*?

Mabel (*shaken*) No—I don't. You don't know *nothing* about me, Lucy Rickworth.

Lucy (*with a cruel smile*) Don't I? I bet I know more than Somerset House does.

Mabel (*trying to bluff*) Huh . . . (*She looks around at everyone's faces*)

What are you lot gawping at? Have I got two heads, or something?
(*She bridles*) Anyway—I can't stop here all day wasting time. Some
folks have work to do. (*She moves to the door* R) I—er—I'll p'raps see
you later on, Sam—Joe . . .

Mabel exits rapidly

Sam (*to Lucy*) What were all that about?
Lucy Oh, nothing important, Sam. But I don't think we'll have any trouble
now Mabel and me understand each other more clearly. (*She sits down
again with a satisfied smile*) I'll have that cup of tea now, if you don't mind.
Sam (*bewildered*) Aye. (*He turns to Joe*) Joe . . .
Joe Coming up.

*Joe pours a cup of tea and crosses to Lucy with it taking the lemon from Sam
as he passes him. He hands Lucy the cup, and as she takes it, drops the
lemon into the cup. Lucy and Reuben stare at it in fascination*

Lucy I could have managed with just a slice.
Joe Oh, sorry. (*He puts his fingers into the cup to get the lemon out and
scalds his fingers*) Owww! (*He sticks his fingers in his mouth*)
Sam (*quickly*) I'll get you another cup, Lucy. (*He takes the cup from her
and scurries to the table with it*)
Reuben Sorry about that set-to, Sam.
Sam (*pouring more tea*) You've no need to be. I've been trying to choke
her off for years. I'll have to get Lucy to give me a few tips.
Reuben Still—she were right about one thing, Sam. I never thought I'd
see the inside of this house again. Not after all the fuss when the engage-
ment were broken off between me and Alice.
Sam (*slicing the lemon*) Aye—well—that's all water under the bridge,
Reuben.
Reuben Still—(*he laughs*)—I'd hate to think what Alice'd be saying if she
could see me now.
Sam (*remembering*) Aye, so do I. (*He takes tea to Lucy and Reuben*)
Reuben (*taking a cup*) By—It were a right shemozzle, that were. You'd
have thought I'd robbed the Bank of England instead of just having
the nerve to propose to Dan Hardacre's only unwedded daughter before
asking his permission first. (*He sips his tea and chuckles*)
Sam He were a funny old devil from all accounts.
Reuben He were an' all. O' course, you never knew him, did you, Sam?
Old Dan. A right old—(*he glances at Lucy*)—gentleman, he were.
Temper like a gorilla—*and* looked like one.
Lucy Reuben.
Reuben Well, he *did*. Worked down Fryston Colliery pulling coal tubs. He
could shift more tubs than five ponies could—and in half the time. He
dropped dead of heart attack one afternoon—about two weeks after
he'd made me break the engagement off. (*He sips his tea*)
Sam (*startled*) Eh? You mean—it were him what *made* you do it? It
weren't because you *wanted* to?

Joe He forced you?

Reuben (*chuckling*) Threatened to break me in half if I so much as looked at her again. I weren't as big in them days, and he ate youngsters like me for breakfast. No, I took me ring back wi'out having to be told twice.

Sam (*stunned*) Well by heck. And all these years . . .

Reuben I know. Alice's been blaming it on me. She thought I didn't have the guts to stand up to him and fight for her—and she were right. She never forgave me for it.

Sam You don't have to tell *me* that. When our Terry let on it were your Susan he were wanting to marry, she nearly went through the roof.

Reuben I'll bet.

Joe But what stopped you from going back to her after the old man had died?

Reuben Well, I'd met Lucy, by that time and realized what a mistake I'd nearly made. (*He smiles at Lucy*) I couldn't go back to Alice—not then. And that's what *really* put her back up. Knowing that she'd had me and been forced to let me go, and then when the only obstacle had been removed—finding out that I didn't *want* to go back—well—I can imagine how she must have felt.

Sam Aye. (*His forehead creases in a frown*)

Reuben I tried to explain things to her, but she wouldn't listen. She just slammed the door in my face. I couldn't understand it. It all seemed so out of character with her—you know—all *wrong*. She'd sort of—changed.

Sam Aye—I found that out as well—only it were too late for me.

Reuben You don't mind me telling you all this, do you, Sam? I mean, I've not been able to say anything before . . .

Sam No, no. Of course not. No—it's cleared up quite a few things that had me puzzled. (*He shakes his head*) Only—if that were all—then . . . (*He shrugs helplessly*)

Reuben Then what?

Sam Oh, never mind. It doesn't matter. (*He smiles*)

Lucy Well if you two have finished reminiscing, could I have another cup of tea, please?

Joe (*jumping to it*) I'll get it. (*He goes for Lucy's cup*)

Lucy (*smiling*) And I'll not take so much lemon in it, this time, Mr Gittings. (*She hands the cup to him*)

Joe (*wryly*) No. (*He moves back to the table with the cup*)

The door R *opens and Alice glides in, closing the door behind her*

Only Sam sees her. He reacts. She stands there silently gazing at Lucy and Reuben

Lucy (*shivering*) Oh—I've suddenly gone all cold.

Reuben Somebody walking over your grave, love?

Sam reacts

Lucy Feels like they're dancing on it. (*She laughs merrily*)
Joe (*pouring*) You must be sitting in a draught, Lucy. There's lots of 'em in these older houses, isn't there, Sam? (*No answer*) Sam?
Sam (*gazing in horror at Alice*) Eh?
Joe Draughts.
Sam (*his eyes still fixed on Alice*) No—no. I—er—I've got a pack of playing cards if you like . . .

Lucy laughs

Reuben (*grinning*) Come on, Sam. Snap out of it.
Sam (*still watching Alice*) Eh? (*He blinks and looks at Reuben*) Oh, sorry— I—er—I were daydreaming. (*His eyes go back to Alice*)
Lucy That's a sign of old age creeping on—(*coyly*)—so I'm told. I thought for a minute you'd seen a ghost.
Sam (*startled*) What? (*He looks at Lucy*)
Lucy You went so white. (*concerned*) You are all right, aren't you?
Sam (*gulping*) Aye. Aye, I'm all right—for the minute.
Reuben I should sit down if I were you, Sam. You still look a bit unsteady. It must have been a bit of a strain for you this last week or two, what with Alice, an' all. Come on. Sit yourself down and relax.
Joe (*moving to Lucy with her tea*) Aye—that's what I keep telling him. Relax and forget about it.
Lucy (*taking the cup*) Well—it's easy to say it, Mr Gittings, but it's not so easy to do it. (*To Sam*) I bet in spite of everything you miss her, don't you?

Joe moves back to the table

Sam (*still eyeing Alice*) Not as much as I'd like to.
Lucy (*patting the sofa beside her*) Come on, Sam. Sit down next to me. (*To Reuben*) Shove over, Reuben.

Reuben grins and rises, moving to the fireside. Sam sits cautiously beside Lucy, keeping his eyes fixed on Alice, who remains standing by the door

There, that's better, isn't it? All nice and friendly like. Just like we should have been all these years. (*She smiles*) Now then, Sam . . . (*She notices his peculiar position*) Have you got a stiff neck?
Sam Eh? (*He realizes*) Oh—no. No, I—er—I'm all right, thanks. (*He faces her with a weak smile*)
Lucy (*glancing at Reuben questioningly*) Well—I'd just like to say—on behalf of us both—me and Reuben—how *glad* we are that our Susan's got herself engaged to your Terry.
Reuben She couldn't have found a better lad.

Alice moves to the middle of the room, Sam's eyes following her

Lucy They're going to be *so* happy.
Alice That's what *she* thinks.
Lucy She'll be a good wife to him, Sam, so you don't have to worry. I've been teaching her to cook the same as me. (*She simpers*)

Alice In that case he'd be lucky to get through the first week without food poisoning.

Lucy After all, Sam. You know what they say? The way to a man's heart is through his stomach. (*She pokes Sam playfully*)

Joe Aye, that's true, Lucy. It were t' first thing that attracted me to my Renee, that were. She were a first-class cooker.

Alice (*sniffing*) She couldn't boil water without burning it.

Lucy (*eyes wide*) Was she really, Mr Gittings? I always think it's *so* important in a marriage to be able to cook well, don't you?

Joe Aye. She could have written a book on cooking, could my Renee.

Alice Yes. "A Thousand and One ways of Opening a Tin". (*To Sam*) Are you going to get rid of this lot—or shall *I* do it?

Sam (*hissing*) Go away.

Lucy (*startled*) Pardon?

Sam (*recovering*) I—er—I said—it's a lovely day.

Lucy Oh—yes—beautiful. (*She looks puzzled*)

Alice Well?

Sam (*to Lucy*) Do—er—do you fancy going for a walk?

Reuben (*surprised*) Walk?

Reuben and Lucy look at each other

Lucy (*with a half smile*) Where to?

Alice Anywhere—so long as you don't come back here.

Sam (*quickly*) I don't mind. Just—a walk.

Lucy (*uncertain*) Well—if you like. (*She glances at Reuben again and rises*)

Reuben I'll get the coats then, shall I? (*He moves to the door* L)

Lucy I—I'd better powder me nose then. (*To Sam*) Is the bathroom upstairs?

Sam Second door on the left.

Lucy gives him a quick smile and exits L *followed by Reuben. The door closes behind them*

Joe (*puzzled*) What's wi' the idea of a walk, Sam?

Sam (*urgently*) She's here. Alice. (*He points at her*)

Joe (*following the direction of Sam's finger*) Oh? (*He looks at Sam*) Er—are you *sure*?

Sam Of course I'm sure. She's standing right there. I can see her. She says I've got to get them out of here—or she will.

Joe (*uncertainly*) You're not dreaming this, are you? I mean—you really can see her?

Sam (*howling*) I've told you . . .

Joe moves forwards, arms outstretched, and touches Alice

Joe I can't feel anything.

Sam Of course you can't, you fool. There's nothing there to feel.

Alice (*grimly*) If he doesn't keep his filthy nicotine-stained fingers to himself, I shall tear his arm out by the roots and beat him to death with the soggy end of it. I'm not having him messing about inside my lungs. I might catch something.

Sam (*to Alice*) Now just you listen to me for a minute . . .

Joe gapes at Alice and Sam

Alice No. You listen to me. As soon as them two get back in here, you can tell 'em to take their hooks. Their Susan's not marrying our Terry and that's final. Understand?

Sam No, I don't. There's more to this than meets the eye, and I'm going to get to the bottom of it. Our Terry *is* going to marry that lass, and there's nothing you can do about it. So you can stick that up your shroud!

Reuben enters L. *He wears his coat and carries Lucy's*

Reuben Well, *I'm* ready. Lucy'll be down in a minute.

Sam Take that coat off, Reuben. I've changed me mind. We're stopping in.

Reuben Eh?

Alice (*warningly*) Sam . . .

Sam (*loudly*) Get knotted!

Reuben You what?

Sam (*quickly*) Getting hotter—too hot for walking. (*He grins weakly*)

Reuben (*doubtfully*) Oh—aye . . .

Lucy enters L *beaming*

Lucy All right? (*She glances round at everyone*)

Joe We—er—we're not going out after all, Lucy.

Lucy (*surprised*) Oh? (*She glances at Reuben oddly*)

Sam (*laughing falsely*) No. It's too hot, you see. I—er—thought perhaps we'd better have another cup of tea instead. (*To Joe*) Put the kettle on, will you, Joe?

Joe Aye.

Joe hurries off R

Alice Get them out of here, Sam.

Sam (*ignoring her*) Sit down, Lucy—Reuben . . . (*He ushers them to the sofa*)

Alice If they haven't gone in two minutes, you'll regret it.

Sam (*ignoring her*) Iced bun, anybody? (*He hurries back to the table*)

Lucy Well, I wouldn't say no . . . (*She looks at Reuben for his reply*)

Alice No, I bet you wouldn't. Well, try these for flavour.

As Sam turns, the plate of iced buns in his downstage hand, Alice grabs his wrist, forces him to take a bun and swings him to face Lucy and Reuben squarely

One, two, three.

Sam (*puzzled*) One, two, three?

Alice hurls Sam's hand and the bun flies at Lucy. Before Sam realizes what is happening, she has, using his hand, thrown three of them at the seated couple. The buns hit them. Lucy yelps, Reuben stands

Reuben Hey . . . ?

Sam (*tearing his hand free of Alice's grip*) Oh! Oh, no. (*He dashes over to Lucy*) Oh, Lucy—I'm ever so sorry. They—they slipped out of my fingers. Honestly—I'm ever so sorry.

Lucy (*brushing herself down angrily*) That's—all right, Sam. Accidents will happen. (*She glares at him*)

Sam (*scrabbling about on the floor picking up the buns*) Yes—yes. I'm sorry. I'm awfully sorry. Both of you. (*He puts the buns on the sofa beside Lucy as he gets them*) I wouldn't have had that happen for the world.

Reuben No—no. (*He brushes himself down warily*)

Sam (*standing*) Sit down, Reuben. I'll get you some fresh ones.

Reuben I—er—I think I'll stand up for a minute, Sam.

Alice (*moving behind Sam and taking his arms*) He said *sit*! (*She pushes Sam's arms forward into Reuben's chest*)

Reuben sits suddenly

Sam (*startled*) Ooh. (*He looks at his arms in horror*)

Reuben (*a little annoyed*) Here . . .

Sam (*quickly*) Sorry, Reuben—I didn't mean to push you so hard. (*He laughs nervously*) Don't know me own strength, do I?

Reuben glowers

I'll get you the buns. (*He looks round for the others*)

Lucy Something wrong?

Alice moves behind the sofa

Sam The buns . . . (*He realizes*) Oh, no. (*He looks at Reuben*)

Reuben's face changes as he realizes he is sitting on something. He rises and turns to look

Lucy (*horrified*) Reuben—all over your trousers.

Reuben glares fiercely at Sam

Sam (*wincing*) Sorry.

Reuben My best suit.

Sam (*galvanized into action*) Hold on—hold on.

Sam spins to the table, grabs a knife and advances on Reuben to scrape the icing off him

Reuben (*retreating*) Oh, no you don't. (*He turns to Lucy*) Lucy . . .

Lucy (*snatching the knife from Sam*) He's just had this cleaned, as well. (*She scrapes savagely at the icing*)

Sam (*almost in tears*) I'm ever so sorry.

Reuben You're not as sorry as I am. What's up with you? (*He lets out a yell of pain as Lucy scrapes a bit fiercely*) Owww—steady on!

Lucy (*snapping*) Well hold still, then.

Sam It was an accident.

Lucy (*balefully*) Yes.

Alice Want me to go on, Sam?

Sam I'll go get a cloth. (*He dashes towards the door* R. *As he passes Alice he mutters*) Just you try it.

Sam exits R

Alice Well then . . . (*She looks around*)

Lucy (*glancing at the closing door*) He did that on purpose, Reuben. Threw them buns. He did it on *purpose*, I tell you.

Reuben Nay, love—he'd got no call to do that. It were an accident.

Lucy It wasn't. (*She puts the knife down on the sofa arm*) I saw him do it. He took deliberate aim.

Reuben But what for? Why should he do that?

Lucy (*snapping*) How the devil do I know—but he did.

Sam enters R *with a damp cloth*

Sam Here you are—a damp cloth. That should do it. (*He holds it out*)

Alice How right you are.

Alice takes the cloth suddenly and wraps it round Lucy's face. Lucy squarks

Lucy (*clawing the cloth away*) Reuben. *Reuben!* (*She flings it away*)

Sam Lucy . . .

Reuben It's all right, love. I saw him that time.

Sam No—it wasn't—I mean . . .

Reuben I don't know what's gotten into you, Sam, but you can just cut it out. Understand. We've had enough.

Sam Reuben—Lucy—listen to me . . .

Lucy (*standing*) Reuben—get my coat.

Sam Wait. Don't go . . .

Joe enters R *with a large trifle in a bowl*

Joe (*cheerfully*) One bowl of trifle.

Alice Aha . . .

Joe Where does it go?

Alice I'll show you. (*She moves towards Joe*)

Sam (*howling*) No! (*He flings himself at Joe and grabs the bowl*)

Lucy and Reuben stare at each other and Sam

Alice Hand it over, Sam. (*She holds out her hands*)

Sam Keep away. (*He clutches it to him*)

Lucy (*to Reuben*) He's gone mad.

Sam (*to Alice*) You nasty-tempered old faggot.

Lucy (*indignant*) I beg your pardon?

Reuben I warned you, Sam . . .

Alice Don't you call me names, Sam Early.

Sam Reuben—Lucy—listen. You don't understand. It isn't me that's doing all this—it's Alice. It's all Alice.

Lucy Alice? (*She looks at Reuben*)

Sam Yes—she's come back to haunt me. Stop our Terry getting wed to your Susan. She's right here, now—right there. (*He indicates her with his head*)

Joe Sam . . .

Lucy (*backing away*) Reuben—my coat. Quick.

Reuben (*watching Sam*) Aye . . . (*He picks up Lucy's coat*)

Sam Don't go. Don't walk out on me.

Alice Give me the trifle, Sam.

Sam (*shouting*) No—keep back. You're not having it. No. No. (*He scurries round the sofa to the lower edge of the fireplace*)

Lucy (*squealing*) Look out—he's going to throw it at us. (*She crouches behind Reuben*) Reuben!

Reuben flings his arms up to hide his face

The door L *opens, and Susan and Terry enter*

Terry Hello? (*He sees the picture*) What's happening?

Susan Mother?

Lucy (*staggering to her feet*) Susan—get out of here, quick.

Susan But why? What's happening?

Reuben (*lowering his arms and turning to her*) Never mind. Don't ask questions. Just go.

Terry (*to Sam*) What is it?

Sam It's your mother again.

Terry Oh, no. (*His face creases with anguish*)

Lucy (*to Susan*) I thought I told you to go.

Susan But Mother . . .

Sam Reuben—you don't understand . . .

Reuben Yes I do, Sam. I understand perfectly. You've gone off your nut. You're balmy.

Sam (*horror-struck*) No . . .

Reuben Yes. And if you think we're going to let our Susan marry your Terry after this little lot, then you've got another think coming.

Sam But it's not my fault.

Reuben Susan—give Terry his ring back.

Joe Here—just a minute . . .

Reuben You stay out of it, Joe. I'm having no insanity in my family.

Terry What do you mean, insanity? There's nothing wrong with me.

Lucy That's what we thought to start with, but it hasn't taken us long to find out different. I'm sorry, Terry. It's not you personally, but we can't take the risk. You might end up as daft as your dad.

Sam Lucy . . .

Lucy If you take my advice, Sam, you'll see a doctor as soon as possible.

Sam But there's nothing wrong with me.

Reuben That's what they all say. Come on, Susan . . .

Terry Wait . . .

Lucy Give him his ring, Susan.

Susan But Mum . . .

Lucy NOW!

Susan slowly takes off the ring

Terry Dad—say something.

Alice turns away

Reuben (*taking the ring*) Here's your ring, Terry. (*He holds it out to him*)

Terry I don't want the rotten ring. I want Susan. (*He pushes it aside*)

Reuben Well you can't have her. Now come on, Susan—Lucy—I think we'd better be going. (*He puts the ring on the table*)

Lucy and Reuben move to the door L

Terry (*helplessly*) Susan.

Susan Don't worry, Terry. I'll talk them round.

Lucy (*sharply*) Susan.

Reuben opens the door L

Susan (*to Terry*) 'Bye . . .

    Susan is pulled out by Lucy, and Reuben follows

Terry (*to Sam, furiously*) Now look what you've done. You've made them break off the engagement.

Sam It were nothing to do with me, lad. It's your mother.

Terry Don't give me all that again, Dad. I'm fed up with it. I don't know what you did, but you've really succeeded in messing up my life now.

Sam Terry . . .

Terry Well you won't get the chance to do it again because I'm getting out. And if you take my advice you'll do as Mrs Rickworth told you and get yourself off to the doctor's for some treatment, because in my opinion, you're badly in need of it. I'll go pack me things.

    Terry exits L

Alice (*turning*) Sam—you're not going to let him go like that, are you? Stop him.

Sam (*distraught*) Oh you keep out of this. You've done enough damage for one day.

Joe Eh?

Sam (*brokenly*) No, not you, Joe—her.

Joe (*helplessly*) Do you want me to go after him, then?

Alice (*to Joe*) Of course he does. Stop him. He can't leave home like this.

Sam What's the use, Joe. He won't listen.

Alice *Make* him listen. Sam! *Sam!*

Joe Is she still here? (*He looks round*)

Sam Aye . . . (*He indicates Alice listlessly*)

Joe (*to Alice*) I suppose you feel quite proud of yourself now, you old flea-bag. You've done what you set out to do, haven't you?

Alice sweeps over to the door L, *her face grim. Joe carries on speaking to where she was*

Well, all I hope is that when it's time for me to go, I'll be able to find you and make things as hot for you as you're making 'em for this poor chap here.

Alice (*shaking*) Tell him to keep quiet, Sam.

Joe Call yourself a woman? You never were a woman. You were a monster. Driving him like a dray horse, night and day, nivver giving him any peace——

Alice Sam . . .

Joe —year in, year out till the day you died. Well just let me tell you this much, Alice Early. You're dead for a lot longer than you are alive, and by heck, won't you know about it when I arrive over there.

Alice (*anxiously*) Sam . . .

Sam Go on. Take your hook. Leave us alone. I just don't want to set eyes on you ever again.

Alice (*sniffing*) All this fuss over a broken engagement. It's not the end of the world, is it? He'll come back, Sam. I know he will. As soon as he's calmed down a bit.

Sam Get out.

Alice is about to say something further, then thinks better of it, and turns to the door L

And don't come back.

Alice (*with venom*) I'm not going anywhere. I've told you. I'm staying right here where I belong. This is still my house and don't you ever forget it.

Alice exits quickly L

Sam (*quietly*) She's gone.

Joe So—what are you going to do now, Sam?

Sam (*sitting on the sofa and cradling the trifle bowl*) I don't know, Joe—I just don't know.

Sam's head drops forward. Joe looks at him helplessly as—

the CURTAIN *falls*

SCENE 2

The same. The following Saturday, early evening

The room is almost unchanged since the previous week. The table has been cleared, and the vase of flowers stands on it once more. A small tray is on the corner of the table, and on it is a teapot, milk jug, sugar bowl and spoon. The rest of the room is tidy. The light outside is fading fast but the curtains are still unclosed

Sam sits on the sofa, almost in the same position as at the end of the last scene, a mug of tea between his hands, eyes unseeing. After a moment, the door L opens cautiously and Mabel enters

Mabel (*quietly*) Sam. (*No reaction*) Sam?

Sam (*snapping out of his daydream*) Eh? (*He turns his head*) Oh—it's you. (*He looks down again*)

Mabel (*moving behind him*) You—er—you don't mind me coming round, do you? (*No answer*) Only I haven't seen you since last week when Lucy and Reuben were here, so I wondered if everything was all right. (*Silence*) Is it?

Sam (*dully*) Eh?

Mabel All right?

Sam All right, what?

Mabel Everything.

Sam Oh. Yes—yes—it's all right.

Mabel If there's anything you want . . . (*She stops and looks at him*)

Sam No. No thanks.

Mabel Anything at all. I mean—you just have to say so, and I'll . . .

Sam (*snapping*) I said no, didn't I?

Mabel No need to snap me head off. I were only trying to be helpful.

Sam (*sighing*) I'm sorry, Mabel. I just don't feel like company at the minute.

Mabel Oh, come on, Sam. Snap out of it. It's not like you to be like this.

Sam Well how do you expect me to be? Dancing on the tabletop? Our Terry's left home and I don't know where he is—and Lucy and Reuben Rickworth won't even let me *try* to explain about what happened here last week. I never thought I'd see you round here again either, come to think of it.

Mabel (*wryly*) Well—I suppose I'd only got meself to blame. I shouldn't have been so confounded nosey. (*She gives a nervous laugh*) That's my trouble, you know. I like to be in on everything.

Sam I can't say I hadn't noticed.

Mabel I suppose not. Is it all right if I sit down?

Sam Help yourself.

Mabel (*sitting*) Any chance of a cup of tea?

Sam (*glancing up*) Why? What's up?

Mabel Nothing—only—well, I'd like to have a word with you.

Sam If it's about that set-to last Sunday . . . (*He rises and moves to the sideboard for a cup, then goes to the table*)

Mabel It's not—well—in a way it is. I've been having a word with Joe Gittings.

Sam (*pouring*) Joe? I thought you two weren't on speaking terms?

Mabel I've lost count of the times Joe Gittings and me haven't been on speaking terms, but we can always find summat to say to each other.

Sam brings the cup to Mabel and she takes it

Sit down, Sam.

Sam sits

Now then . . . (*She sips her tea*)

Sam Well?

Mabel He told me what's been happening in here.

Sam (*rising*) All right, Mabel, you've had your fun. The joke's over. Just finish your tea and——

Mabel Oh, sit down and shut up, Sam. I've not come to laugh at you, you big booby. Now sit down and listen a minute.

Sam hesitates, and then sits again

I had to ask him what had been going on because just as you got to the interesting part last Sunday afternoon, the end of me stethoscope broke off and I missed . . . (*She sees Sam's face and stops speaking*) Oh—yes—well . . . Oh, what's it matter. It's out now. I were listening through the wall with it. Our Eustace got it in a jumble sale for me. That's how I knew so much of what was going on round here. Anyway—Joe told me all about Alice and the way she's been carrying on.

Sam And you believed him, did you?

Mabel Why shouldn't I? It's the only thing that'd account for the daft way you've been behaving these last couple of weeks. And besides—I saw her myself, if you remember? (*She sips her tea*)

Sam Aye—aye, I do.

Mabel I knew it weren't no plastic sheeting I'd seen out there. No. It were her all right. Come back to stop your Terry getting wed, so Joe tells me.

Sam Aye—and it looks like she's managed it, doesn't it?

Mabel I wouldn't say that, Sam—not yet, anyway.

Sam What do you mean?

Mabel (*glancing around her nervously*) She—er—she's not in here with us now, is she?

Sam No.

Mabel Gone away, has she?

Sam No such luck. She's upstairs making the beds and dusting.

Mabel Eh?

Sam She's been doing the housework all week. Cooking meals, doing the washing. It's unnerving, that's what it is. Having a ghost running round after you all the time.

Mabel Running around after you? Alice?

Sam I know. I can't understand it, but she says it gives her something to do while she's waiting.

Mabel Waiting for what?

Sam Our Terry to come back, I suppose. I don't know. We're not on speaking terms. Anyway, it looks like she'll be here for quite a while yet. Our Terry won't set foot in this house again—not till he's got Susan back—and there's fat chance of that ever happening after last Sunday's little episode.

Mabel Oh, I don't know, Sam. It could be arranged.

Sam How?

Mabel Ways and means.

Sam Anyway—why should you bother? I thought you didn't like the Rickworths.

Mabel I don't. Nasty, stuck up pieces, they are ...

Sam Well then?

Mabel I found something out last week, Sam. Something I didn't know anybody else knew about. Not around here, anyroad.

Sam Oh?

Mabel You'll not say anything, will you? If I tell you.

Sam No, if you don't want me to.

Mabel It's about me and Fred Sutton.

Sam What about you?

Mabel (*after a slight pause*) We weren't wed. Never were.

Sam Eh?

Mable (*quickly*) You're not shocked, are you, Sam? You don't mind?

Sam (*shrugging*) It's nowt to do with me, Mabel. Except ... What about your Eustace and Denise?

Mabel (*grimacing*) Aye.

Sam That makes 'em just a couple of ...

Mabel (*quickly interrupting*) I know.

Sam (*wondering*) And to think of the times I've called ... (*He coughs*) But—er—what's all this got to do with the Rickworths?

Mabel Well—it were *her*, you see—Lucy Rickworth. What she said to me last Sunday. You remember? She called me—Holdsworth, didn't she?

Sam What's wrong wi' that? It's your name, isn't it? I mean ... before you were—well—supposed to be—married.

Mabel No. I were born Mabel Tonkinson, and Clem Holdsworth were the feller I married when I were seventeen. It didn't work out, so I left him to live over the brush with Fred Sutton. So now you know, Sam. I'm just a common old tally-woman. (*She looks down*)

Sam I see—and Lucy knew about it?

Mabel Aye. I could have sworn nobody round here knew but *she* did. And all these years she's kept her mouth shut. Oh, Sam, I could have died for shame when I realized. If I'd have been her ...

Sam (*nodding*) I can imagine.

Mabel It'd have been all over Castleford. So that was it. I've been brood-
ing on it all week, and I want to make up for all I've said about her this
last few years.

Sam So why come round here?

Mabel Well, after I'd talked to Joe, I thought I might be able to help get
your Terry and their Susan back together again.

Sam Fat chance of that. I don't even know where he is.

Mabel But I do. He's staying down Lock Lane at that Nugent lad's. He's
been there all week.

Sam How did you find that out?

Mabel I met Mrs Nugent last night at bingo, and she told me.

Sam (*eagerly*) How is he?

Mabel Still upset. He went up to Rickworth's the other day, but they
wouldn't let him see her.

Sam (*nodding*) So what do you think *you* can do about it? I shouldn't think
they'll be wanting to see you either.

Mabel No—that's what I thought—but I decided to take a chance on it,
so I went up to their shop this afternoon. I bought five pounds of tripe.
(*She shudders*) and I can't stand the stuff. Soon as I got home, I tipped
the whole lot straight into the dustbin.

Sam What did they say?

Mabel Well—they were a bit off, as you can imagine, but—well—I hope
you don't mind, Sam—I've asked 'em to come down here tonight and
see you.

Sam You've done *what*?

Mabel (*quickly*) They're coming as soon as they've finished in the shop.

Sam (*rising and moving to the fire*) What the devil did you want to go and
do that for, Mabel? Why can't you mind your own business? Aren't
things bad enough as they are?

Mabel I suppose so—but you've not heard the rest of it yet. I sent a
message to your Terry as well.

Sam (*aghast*) You've not told him to come?

Mabel (*nodding*) And Joe Gittings.

Sam (*helplessly*) Why didn't you ask the Mayor while you were at it?

Mabel (*puzzled*) I think he's got a reception on tonight. But if you like . . .

Sam What good will it do? Having everybody down here?

Mabel Well—I want you to explain to 'em all exactly what's been happening.

Sam Explain? You must be joking. They'll never believe me.

Mabel Yes they will—and remember—*I've* seen her as well.

Sam And how do you think Alice's going to react to it all? Just stand
there with her mouth open and say nothing? She'll go berserk.

Mabel I'm hoping she will. In fact I'm counting on it.

Sam (*clutching his head*) Oh lor . . .!

Mabel Well don't just stand there. We've got to get things sidened up
before they all arrive. (*She rises and moves to the table*) I'll wash these
and make some fresh. (*She picks up the tray and moves to the door* R)
Pass me that mucky cup o' yours, and tidy them cushions.

Sam gives her his cup silently

   Mabel exits R

Sam gives the cushion a half-hearted thump

Sam Interfering old busybody . . .

   The door L *opens and Terry enters quietly. He wears his jeans, sweater
   and jacket*

Terry Dad.
Sam (*turning*) Terry. (*He moves to him*)
Terry I got your message.
Sam Message? (*He remembers*) Oh—oh, aye. The message.
Terry Well?
Sam Er—come in, lad. Sit down. The—er—the others'll be here in a bit
   I expect.
Terry Others?
Sam Susan—and Mr and Mrs Rickworth.
Terry Rickworths? You mean they're coming here?
Sam That's what I wanted to see you about. I'm going to try and put
   things right for you.
Terry Look, Dad—before you say anything—do you mind if I have a
   word with them first? There's something I've . . .
Sam (*quickly*) You don't have to worry, lad. It'll be all right. You'll have
   that ring back on her finger before tonight's out.
Terry But Dad . . .
Sam (*grasping his shoulder*) Eh, Terry lad. I'm glad you've come back. I've
   been missing you.
Terry Aye. (*He breaks away gently and sits on the sofa*)
Sam I'll explain everything to 'em. Right on the line. They'll be practising
   the *Wedding March* before they leave here this eve.
Terry Maybe, but I'm warning you, Dad. If you so much as mention
   me mother's name while they're here, I'm going to walk out of here for
   good. Understand? No mother—and no ghosts.
Sam Oh.

   Joe enters L

Joe Hey up, there. (*He sees Terry*) Oh, hello, young 'un. You've come back
   then, I see?
Terry For the minute.
Joe (*to Sam*) What's to do with the summons then?
Sam Oh—it—er—it's nothing urgent, Joe. Just a little get together, that's
   all.
Terry It's urgent to *me*.
Sam Oh, aye—aye—er—sit down, Joe.

Joe (*sitting next to Terry*) What's it all in aid of, then?

Sam Well . . . it were Mabel's idea.

Joe I might have guessed she'd have her nose in it somewhere. And what's she want in return?

Mabel enters R *with a tray of crockery, sugar bowl and lemon slices in a dish, just in time to hear the last remark*

Mabel She doesn't want anything, Joe Gittings. She's just trying to make up for a few years of doing the wrong things, that's all.

Joe (*sheepishly*) Hello, Mabel.

Mabel (*moving to the table*) There's no need to look so sheepish. I bet you've said far worse about me in the past. (*She puts the tray down*) Now listen. Before anybody else gets here—and that includes you-know-who—I've got something to say to you, Sam. As soon as we're all together, I want you to start at the beginning and tell us the whole story—start to finish. And don't leave a thing out

Sam (*glancing at Mabel*) But Mabel . . .

Mabel It's the only way, and if I know anything about it, your . . . (*She notices the milk jug is missing*) Oh, I've forgotten the milk jug. Be a love, Terry and go and get it for me.

Terry rises and exits R

Now where was I? Oh, yes. If I know anything about it . . .

Sam Mabel. I can't do it. I can't tell 'em.

Mabel Eh? Why not?

Sam It's Terry. He says that if I so much as mention Alice's name from now on, he's going to walk out of here for good. We'll have to call the whole thing off.

Mabel (*firmly*) Call it off? We'll do no such thing. Not after all the bother I've been to. No—we'll just have to think up some other way, and leave Alice out of it.

Sam That's if she'll stay out. As soon as she finds out what's going on, she'll be downstairs in a shot.

Joe You mean she's still here?

Sam Where else?

Joe Well in that case we'll have to make sure she doesn't come down.

Sam And how do we do that? Slap a "no entry" sign on both doors?

Joe How about rubbing chunks of garlic round the doors and windows?

Mabel That's for vampires, you dope.

Sam Well?

Joe We could always ask the Vicar to come down from Hightown Church.

Sam And what good would that do?

Joe He could get rid of her for you. Permanent, like.

Sam (*interested*) How?

Joe He'll—oh, what's the word? Exorcise—that's it. He'll exorcise her.

Sam (*puzzled*) You mean—take her for a walk?

Mabel No, you daft ha'porth. It's a sort of service they have to get rid of ghosts and things. I've read about it in one of our Denise's books.
Sam You mean—he'll do this service thing and she'll go? Just like that?
Mabel I suppose so. It always works in books.
Sam Well that's it, then. That's all we've got to do. Why didn't you tell me this before?
Mabel I never thought.
Sam I'll go up and get him right away. (*He moves for the door* L)
Mabel There's no time, Sam. They'll be here in a few minutes.
Sam (*desperate*) What are we going to do then?
Mabel I've got it. Listen. As soon as Alice comes in, you tip us the wink, and we'll cover up for anything she might do.
Sam (*doubtfully*) Do you think you can?
Mabel It'll be three against one, won't it?
Sam (*worried*) I suppose so—but—all right. I'll do it. The minute she comes down, I'll signal you.

There is a sharp rapping at the front door off L

Mabel That'll·be them. I'll go put the kettle on. Let 'em in, Sam, but don't say a word till I get back.

Mabel exits R

Joe Shall I do it, Sam?
Sam I think you'd better. If Alice heard that knocking, she'll be half way down the stairs by now, and I don't want her to catch me in that hallway.

Joe exits L

Sam moves nervously down to the fireplace, and fiddles with the ornaments on the mantelpiece

Lucy (*off, coldly*) Good evening, Mr Gittings.
Joe (*off*) Oh, hello—come in, won't you? Through there.

Reuben and Lucy enter L, *followed by Joe. They stand stiffly by the door and Joe sidles round to above the table*

Reuben (*to Sam*) Well?
Sam (*gulping*) Reuben—Lucy. (*He smiles weakly*)
Lucy Mrs Sutton said you wanted to see us?
Sam Aye—that's right. (*He glances at the door*) Won't—er—won't you sit down?

Lucy looks at Reuben, then sits on the chair in the centre of the table, putting her handbag on the table top

Reuben I'll stand, if you don't mind.

Sam Wouldn't you rather sit on the sofa, Lucy? It's more comfortable

Lucy Maybe—but is it as safe?

Sam looks uncomfortable

Reuben Well get on with it, Sam. We haven't all night to waste.

Sam Would you like a cup of tea? Mabel's just making some.

Lucy (*coldly*) Not for me, thank you. I just want to know what you want and then we'll be off.

Sam She won't be long.

Lucy If you'll pardon my saying so, Mr Early, I don't see why we have to wait for Mrs Sutton. I hardly think that this'll have anything to do with her.

Sam Well—no—but it's just that I want to tell you both about last Sunday.

Reuben We already know about last Sunday, Sam. We were here. Remember?

Joe (*quickly*) Aye—but he wants to explain things.

Lucy That'll take some doing, I can assure you.

Mabel enters R *with the teapot and milk jug*

Mabel Quicker than I thought, wasn't I? Your Terry already had the kettle on for us. (*She goes to the table*) Hello, Lucy—Reuben.

Reuben Hello.

Mabel Cup of tea, Lucy?

Lucy No thank you.

Mabel (*pouring*) One sugar and a twist of lemon, I think it is. Right? There's nothing like a nice cup of tea, is there? (*She hands it to Lucy*) Reuben?

Reuben Well . . .

Mabel I thought you would. (*She pours out a cup of tea*)

Reuben Now listen . . .

Mabel No sugar for you, I expect? That right, Lucy? Mustn't let him put any more weight on, must we? (*She hands the cup to Reuben*) Oh, don't bother about me, Sam. You go right ahead and tell them.

Sam (*heavily*) Aye . . .

Mabel I should sit down if I were you, Reuben. There's a chair round the other side of Lucy

Reuben sits on the chair below the table

Well, go on, Sam.

Sam Well, it's like this . . . (*He stops*)

Reuben Go on.

Sam I know that what happened here last Sunday must have seemed a bit odd to you—but there's a perfectly reasonable explanation.

Reuben And what's that?

Sam I'm trying to think of it. (*He glances at Mabel*)

Mabel smiles and nods

Lucy Well? We're waiting.

Sam Well, I've been under a bit of a strain these last few weeks . . .

Mabel (*to Lucy*) Losing Alice, you know.

Sam And to cut a long story short—I've not been quite meself.

Lucy I'll not say we hadn't noticed the fact.

Sam I've been seeing things that aren't there.

Reuben We'd noticed that as well.

Sam Well, what I wanted to say to you is this. What's been happening to me—well—it's just been happening to *me*. It's got nothing to do with our Terry. So I want to ask you to let the kids get engaged again. What do you say?

Lucy And is that it? What you wanted to see us about?

Sam Aye.

Lucy (*rising*) Come on, Reuben.

Reuben rises

The door R *opens and Terry enters with a plate of bread and buttered scones*

Terry (*seeing the Rickworths*) Hello. (*He looks round*) Where's Susan?

Reuben We thought it best not for her to come in, lad. She's sitting outside in the car.

Terry Can I see her?

Lucy I'd rather you didn't, if you don't mind. We don't want her more upset than she is already. She's driven me mad this last week with her sniffing and sobbing. Silly little fool.

Reuben I'm sorry, lad. You'll realize it's for the best in time.

Terry But Mr Rickworth . . .

Reuben Good-bye, Sam. Terry.

The door L *opens and Susan comes in*

Terry Susan.

Lucy (*snapping at her*) I told you to wait in the car, didn't I?

Susan (*moving to Terry*) Terry, I had to come.

Reuben (*sharply*) Susan. Do as your mother told you.

Susan (*turning*) I won't, Dad. We're in love. I want to marry him.

Lucy And I've told you you're not going to. You'll marry that lad over my dead body.

Sam (*wincing*) Here we go again.

Susan But Mother . . .

Lucy But nothing. Reuben, tell her.

Terry Mr Rickworth, listen . . .

Lucy No. There's been enough said. It's over with. Finished. And that's that. (*To Susan*) Come on, you, and wait till I get you home.

Terry (*desperately*) Dad . . .

Reuben We can understand how you feel, lad, but we think it's best if you don't see each other again.

Joe Look, Reuben—Lucy—I know it's nowt to do with me, but . . .

Lucy As you so rightly put it, Mr Gittings. It's nowt to do with you, so keep your nose out of things that don't concern you. (*She picks up her bag*)

The door L opens and Alice sweeps into the room

Alice What's going on down here? It's like a madhouse. (*She sees the Rickworths*) What are they doing here? Get 'em out, *Now!*

Sam gazes at Alice blankly

Lucy We'll decide what's best for our daughter, and being married into this family isn't what we'd call an ideal match.

Sam jerks into life and nods madly at Mabel who is still standing quietly behind Joe

Mabel (*beaming*) Now that's what I call a right coincidence, that is. You saying that.

Lucy (*turning to her*) I beg your pardon?

Mabel Well—that's just what Alice said to me the day she died. It wouldn't be a good match at all. And she was quite right, wasn't she?

Everybody looks at Mabel

Joe Here—I thought you were on our side?

Mabel On your side? (*Puzzled*) I'm sure I don't know what you mean by that remark, Joe Gittings. All I'm saying is what my dearest friend Alice Early told me on the day she died.

Sam Look—Mabel . . .

Mabel No—she had your best interests at heart, Terry. She hated the idea of you tying yourself down to somebody—well—somebody who wasn't your social equal, so to speak.

Lucy His what? (*She looks at Reuben*)

Alice (*to Sam*) Has she gone mad?

Mabel I didn't quite understand what she meant at the time—but of course I can see it all now. In view of what's happened since.

Lucy Just a minute, Mrs Sutton. Am I understanding you clearly? Are you trying to insinuate that my daughter isn't good enough to marry *him*. (*She points at Terry*)

Mabel (*innocently*) Who? Me?

Lucy Well I'm not talking to the lampshade.

Mabel I'm not insinuating *anything*. You know me, Lucy. If I have anything to say, I come right out and say it. No. I'm just telling you what my friend Alice told me.

Alice Why—the lying . . . I never said anything of the sort.

Sam Mabel . . .

Mabel Oh—you needn't worry, Sam. I'm not going to say any more if it means upsetting your friends—but I must say how happy Alice'd have been if she'd have known that Lucy and Reuben here were in full agreement with her.

Reuben Full agreement with her? We wouldn't agree with Alice Early on *anything*. There's nothing wrong with my daughter and there's nothing wrong with us. We're honest, hardworking folks, and there's nobody can say any different.

Mabel Of course they can't. I quite agree. But as Alice said—it's not every lad who's willing to sink his pride and marry himself to a lass that reeks of tripe whenever he gets near her.

Terry Now just a minute. *I* didn't . . .

Mabel No, no offence, Terry—but you've done the right thing by your mother, and you've had a lucky escape.

Lucy Lucky escape, my foot, Mrs Sutton. I'm not going to have my daughter slighted by a foul-tongued serpent like Alice Early even if she *is* dead and buried.

Sam Cremated.

Lucy (*glaring*) Cremated, then. If they want to get married, then they can . . .

Alice Oh no they can't.

Reuben Just a minute, Lucy . . .

Lucy (*fuming*) No. They'll get married if I've got to drag 'em screaming in chains to the altar. If it's only to spite *her* wherever she is.

Mabel Oh . . . she wouldn't like that, Mrs Rickworth.

Lucy Then she can lump it, the poison-tongued old witch.

Alice (*pointing at Mabel*) I'll kill her. I'll kill her.

Mabel But you don't understand. It's out of the question for him to marry your Susan now.

Sam Why's that? (*He looks at Mabel in surprise*)

Alice Because I say so—that's why.

Mabel Well, I think he'd better tell you that himself.

All look at Terry

Terry Well—(*he looks at Susan*)—that's what I've been trying to tell you all. I can't marry Susan now—you see—I've just got engaged to somebody else.

Everyone reacts

Mabel That's right. He's taken his mother's last wishes to heart, and he's going to marry somebody of his own social standing.

Alice (*to Sam*) Who's that?

Mabel My daughter Denise.

Everyone gapes

Susan (*aghast*) Terry.

Sam What?

Alice *That* painted hussey?

Terry (*to Susan*) I'm sorry, Susan—that's why I wanted to see you. To explain.

Susan shakes her head in disbelief and backs away

Susan No.

Terry I proposed to her on Wednesday night and she accepted me.

Alice (*shouting at Terry*) You fat-headed feeble-minded—failure.

Susan backs into Reuben's arms

Mabel Isn't anybody going to congratulate him? (*She looks round*)

Sam Oh, blimey. (*He collapses on to the sofa, dazed*)

Reuben But it was only two minutes ago he was saying he was in love with our Susan, here.

Terry I was—I still *am*. It's just that I've decided to do what my mother asked Mabel to tell me—and marry Denise.

Alice (*frothing at the mouth*) Asked her . . .!

Mabel She were always fond of our Denise, Alice were. (*She beams*)

Alice Fond of her? I hated the flaming sight of her.

Lucy (*almost in a shriek*) But he can't. He can't. He's engaged to our Susan.

Joe No he isn't. You made 'em break it off—remember?

Lucy That were a mistake. (*She swings round to Reuben*) Tell him, Reuben. Tell him.

Mabel Too late to do anything about it now, isn't it? He's found somebody better. (*To Sam*) Well, Sam? How do you feel about having me as an in-law?

Alice In-law my foot. He's not going to marry that brazen little tart. Do something, Sam. Stop him.

Sam (*weakly*) Welcome to the family, Mabel.

Mabel Thank you, Sam.

Lucy If he marries your Denise, Mabel Sutton, we'll sue him for breach of promise.

Mabel Just you try it. You'll be laughed out of Court.

Reuben But he can't leave our Susan flat like this. Susan—say something.

Susan (*quietly*) There's nothing left to say.

Terry I'm sorry.

Alice He'll be a lot more sorry when I've finished with him. Stand back. I'm going to materialize. (*She waves her arms furiously*)

Sam (*leaping up*) No!

Everyone stares at him

No. (*To Alice*) Wait.

Alice glowers at him

Just a minute

Lucy Well?

Sam Look—this sort of thing seems to me like—well—like history repeating itself. You, Reuben and Alice—and now Terry, Susan and Denise.

Alice It's nothing of the sort. Sam, listen to me——

Sam (*ignoring her*) Now we all know what happened when we went through this last time—and I don't want to see the same thing happening again—

so will you all go into the kitchen for a minute and let me have a chance
to think things out.

Lucy We can do all the thinking we want to do in here. I say he's got no
right to go and propose——

Reuben Lucy—shut up!

Lucy (*startled*) Eh?

Reuben I said shut up. Sam's right. There's got to be some serious thinking
done if we're going to get this lot sorted out.

Lucy I don't see what——

Reuben *Lucy!*

Lucy shuts up, but glares at Reuben

Mabel I'll show them the way, shall I? Give us a shout when you've
finished—thinking. (*She moves to the door* R, *and winks at Sam behind
Alice's back*) This way, everybody.

Everyone except Sam and Alice exits R

Alice Sam, you've got to stop him. He's not going to——

Sam Sit down!

Alice I beg your pardon?

Sam I said sit.

Alice glares at him, then sits on the sofa

Now just listen to me for a minute, because I've got something to say
to you.

Alice And I've got something to say to you as well. What do you mean
by——

Sam Shut up. I'm doing the talking. It's about time you realized that
you're dead and done with and not needed here any longer.

Alice That's what you think. I'm needed here more now than——

Sam I said shut up!

Alice's mouth closes

Now you can just make up your mind to accept the fact. Our Terry's
going to marry Denise Sutton . . .

Alice *He isn't* . . .

Sam Yes he is—and it's all your fault.

Alice Mine?

Sam Yes, yours. If you'd have let him do what he wanted to do in the
first place, he'd have been marrying Susan Rickworth and we wouldn't
have had all this bother. Well, he's done what you told him, and broken
off his engagement to her.

Alice But he's landed himself with somebody ten times worse. That girl's
as common as sliced bread—and not half as well wrapped.

Sam Well, you've only yourself to blame, and if you try to make him
break it off with Denise, he might find somebody twenty times worse.

Alice That'll take some doing.

Sam Maybe, but if I know our Terry—he'll do it.

Alice I'll not have it. He *can't* marry her.

Sam Then there's only one thing for it, isn't there? He'll have to marry Susan Rickworth.

Alice No.

Sam (*moving away*) Then he'll marry Denise.

Alice (*in anguish*) No. (*She rises*) Oh, all right, then. Let him marry Susan. Let him do what he likes.

Sam (*spinning round*) You mean you'll agree? And you'll leave him alone?

Alice (*miserable*) Yes. Anything to stop him marrying that Denise.

Sam And you'll go away and leave me in peace as well?

Alice No, I—it's . . .

Sam Either you do—or the deal's off.

Alice Oh—all right. I'll go. I'll go.

Sam You mean that?

Alice (*nodding miserably*) Yes.

Sam (*laughing with relief*) Right. I'll call them in and tell him the good news.

Alice Good news.

Alice's face crumples, and she hurriedly exits L

Sam (*going to the door* R *and calling*) It's all right, everybody. Come in. Come on in.

Lucy and Reuben enter and move to the table, Joe and Mabel to the sofa, Susan to the door L, *and Terry to the back of the sofa*

Mabel (*as she seats herself*) Everything all right, now?

Sam (*happily*) All over and done with.

Mabel beams

Lucy (*tartly*) Well?

Sam (*moving to the centre of the room*) In a minute. All in good time. (*He waits till all are settled*) Now then—I've thought things over—and in view of what's passed and what's been said . . .

Reuben Yes?

Sam Well—I think it'll be best all round if our Terry and your Susan get engaged again.

Lucy and Reuben look triumphant

Mabel (*rising*) But what about our Denise?

Reuben She'll have to find herself some other sucker.

Mabel reacts

Lucy (*smirking*) I'm glad you've come to the right decision, Sam. I always knew you had something up top, no matter what Reuben said.

Reuben gapes

Well, don't just stand there, Susan. Aren't you going to give your fiancé a kiss?

Susan (*looking at Terry*) I don't know that I should.

Terry Susan . . .

Lucy Why ever not? (*She looks at Reuben*)

Susan I'm not so sure I want to marry him after all, now. I don't think I could be very happy with a man who'd break off his engagement with one girl and then get engaged to another one in the same week.

Lucy Oh, don't talk so daft, Susan. He only did it because he couldn't have you—(*to Terry*)—didn't you, Terry?

Terry nods

He wasn't in love with *her*. He was going to do it out of duty.

Terry That's right, Susan. I've never loved anybody but you. Ever.

Joe Go on, Susan. Forgive and forget. We all make mistakes.

Lucy Course we do—but now your dad's seen sense at last, there's nothing to stop you. Go on. Kiss and make up.

Susan looks at Terry for a moment, then decides and runs to him. They embrace, and everyone but Mabel beams

(*Smirking*) Come on, Reuben. We'd best get up to our Maggie's and break the good news. (*To Terry and Susan*) We'll see you two later when you come up for air. (*She simpers at everybody*)

Mabel (*glowering*) I bet our Eustace'll have something to say about this. He'll not take kindly to our Denise being chucked over.

Reuben Unless it's over a cliff. Never mind, Mabel. You can't win 'em all.

Sam I—er—I'll see you out, shall I?

Lucy That's all right, Sam. We can find our own way. (*She giggles*)

Reuben P'raps we'll see you in the *Commercial* later on for a drink, Sam?

Sam Aye. Perhaps we will.

Reuben and Lucy exit L, all smiles

Mabel (*as the door closes*) We've done it. (*She leaps around*) We've done it. (*She flings her arms round Terry and Susan*) Congratulations.

Sam (*startled*) Eh?

Joe Are you all right, Mabel?

Mabel (*laughing with Terry*) I never felt better in me life.

Sam But—but what about your Denise? What are you going to tell her?

Mabel What about? The engagement, you mean?

Sam nods

There never was one. Our Denise got herself engaged to that sailor she's been knocking off, nearly two weeks ago.

Joe You mean it were all a put-up job?

Susan (*to Terry*) You weren't engaged at all?

Mabel Tell her, Terry.

Terry (*smiling*) Mrs Sutton came to see me this morning and gave me the full story. At first I wouldn't believe her—after all—it was a bit of a mouthful to swallow—but it was the only thing that explained what had been going on since Mum died. Anyway, she told me what she wanted me to do—and I just played along.

Sam (*to Mabel*) You mean you had all this planned out?

Mabel Down to the last detail.

Sam But why didn't you let on to us? I've been half out of my mind with worry.

Mabel I know, Sam, and I'm sorry—but I couldn't take the risk. If you'd have known what we were up to, Alice'd have tumbled to it like a shot. You never could keep a secret from her, could you?

Sam That's true—but—don't you think you were taking a bit of a risk yourself?

Mabel Not really. You see, I know how a woman's mind works.

Sam I wish I did.

Mabel Anyway, I've done my good deed for the day, so I'll be off. Our Eustace'll be wanting some snap.

Sam I don't know how to thank you, Mabel. I honestly don't.

Mabel I shouldn't bother to try. Things should be back on their old footing by this time next week. Insults flying like feathers.

Sam Nay . . .

Mabel Nay nothing. I'd be disappointed if they weren't. (*She moves to the door* L) Oh, by the way, I wouldn't mind dropping in at the *Commercial* for a milk stout meself, tonight—but don't worry. I'll keep out of sight. Just charge it up to you, eh?

Mabel exits L

Joe Am I invited as well, Sam, or will it be just a selected few?

Sam Joe—it'll be drinks on the house, so if you want one—bring your own bucket.

Joe Nay, I'll do better than that. I've got a tin bath in the outhouse. (*He laughs*)

Terry (*putting his arm around Susan*) We're going down to Brian Nugent's to get the engagement ring from my suit. We'll be back in about an hour and come for a drink with you.

Sam Oh, no you don't. No drinks for you till you're eighteen.

Susan (*smiling*) Does that mean what I think it means, Mr Early?

Sam It means an empty house for a few hours, aye . . .

Terry (*grinning*) Thanks Dad.

Terry and Susan exit L

Joe Well, that's it then, Sam. It's all over.

Sam Aye—no more trouble—and no more Alice.

Joe I'll go get into me drinking togs then. See you in five minutes.

Joe exits L

Sam (*singing*) Pack up all my cares and woe—here I go—cheerio—bye-bye, Alice. (*He picks up the tea-tray*) Where the devil waits for you—fork in hand—shovel too—bye-bye, Alice.

Sam exits R

The door L *opens and Alice enters slowly*

Alice looks around wearily, then picks up the wedding photo. Still carrying it, she moves to the sofa and sits gazing at it. Suddenly her shoulders heave and she begins to sob quietly

Sam enters R, *still singing*

Sam (*singing*) So stoke the fire good and hot—give old Alice all you've got—Alice, bye-bye. (*He sees Alice*) Alice.

Alice sobs a little louder

What are you doing here? I thought you'd gone.
Alice (*looking up, eyes streaming*) I can't. (*She sobs louder*)
Sam What do you mean—you can't? You *promised*.
Alice I know I did—but they won't let me in. (*She sobs even louder*)
Sam Who won't?
Alice Them. (*She sobs*)
Sam You mean—on your side?

Alice nods

But why?
Alice Because of what's happened down here.
Sam How do you mean?
Alice (*sniffling*) It's one of their rules. You can't pass over without a clear conscience.
Sam But you told me before—when you first came back—that you you wouldn't go with them.
Alice (*miserably*) I know. I told you a lie. They wouldn't take me from the start. That's why I came back. I'd nowhere else to go.
Sam Eh? But I thought you came back to stop our Terry getting married.
Alice No.
Sam But you *tried*. You *tried* to stop him.
Alice (*her face crumpling again*) I know.
Sam (*baffled*) Why?
Alice Oh, Sam—I'm so ashamed. (*She sobs*)
Sam (*baffled*) Look, Alice . . .
Alice I couldn't let him marry her, Sam. Not without trying to stop him.
Sam For heaven's sake, *why*? Why?
Alice (*sniffling*) Sit down, Sam—and I'll tell you.
Sam (*sitting beside her*) Well?

Alice You always thought I looked on you as second best, didn't you? Just somebody I'd caught on the rebound from Reuben Rickworth. I always told you he jilted me—but he didn't.

Sam Aye, I know. Your father made him do it. Reuben told me last week.

Alice Yes—but what Reuben didn't know was—I asked me dad to do it.

Sam (*startled*) You what?

Alice I'd seen you, you see—working in Colley's storehouse—and I'd realized that it were you I wanted and Reuben were just a mistake. You were a handsome feller in them days, Sam. (*Quietly*) You still are— (*more firmly*)—and I knew I wanted you more than anything else in the world.

Sam Come off it, Alice. You don't expect me to swallow that, do you?

Alice It's true enough. It took me six weeks to make you notice me. I used to wait for you leaving, every dinner-time, then pretend to be coming from the other direction just so that I could smile at you. I thought you'd *never* ask me out, but when you finally did I was so happy I cried for hours when I got home. That's when I spoke to me dad and he got rid of Reuben for me. Oh, Sam, I were so much in love with you.

Sam You'd a funny way of showing it.

Alice (*sadly*) You never really understood me, did you, Sam? You never knew why I acted the way I did?

Sam That's true. I just collected the bruises. And any road—if this is all true—why did you spent all our married life trying to drive me away from you? You never gave me a minute's peace.

Alice I couldn't afford to. If you'll think about it for a minute, you might see. You used to drink a lot, didn't you, Sam? Nearly all your wages went on beer. I couldn't let that go on, now could I? We *needed* that money—for the furniture and things—and for our Terry. As for the rest of it—well—you weren't too bright a fellow, were you? You let folks take advantage of your good nature. They were always borrowing off you—and never paying back. Making you look a fool and poking fun at you. I had to put a stop to that as well, didn't I? I wanted you to be respected, and I wasn't my father's daughter for nothing—so I did the fighting for you.

Sam If I'd so much wrong with me in the first place then, it beats me what you saw in me.

Alice I've told you, Sam. I loved you—(*quietly*)—and I still do.

Sam (*blinking*) Eh?

Alice Nothing'll alter that, Sam. Despite anything I've ever said or done. I want you to believe that.

Sam Well, what was all this fuss about our Terry and Susan Rickworth? You've still not explained that.

Alice (*hanging her head*) Pride, Sam. Just pride. You know I've always been a proud woman. I was afraid that if he ever *did* marry into their family, he'd somehow find out what had really happened all them years ago.

Sam How could he? Even Reuben didn't know. And in any case—what would it matter?

Alice It mattered to *me*, Sam. I didn't want anybody to know the dirty trick I'd played on Reuben to get you—and both our Ethel and our Doris knew what had really happened. It could have slipped out unintentional like from one of *them*. And after all I'd said about Reuben over the years—I didn't want our Terry to think too badly of me.

Sam Well of all the cock-eyed reasoning. He *couldn't* think any worse of you now—not after these last few weeks.

Alice I know. You needn't rub it in. I was wrong. I admit it. But I'd been making the decisions for so long I just had to go on doing it. I couldn't help meself. I daren't let go of the whip for a minute in case you both realized it were all a front I were putting up. Anyway—I've told you now. You know the whole story. (*She rises*) I just wanted to tell you the truth before I went.

Sam Where are you going to?

Alice I don't know. Nowhere, I suppose. I'll just have to drift around till they've decided what to do about me.

Sam And—how will you know?

Alice They told me I'd hear a little bell. That'd be the signal they'd made their minds up. (*She sniffles*) Good-bye, Sam. I really *am* going this time. You'll not see me again—at least—not till you cross over. (*She moves to the door* L, *head down*)

Sam (*suddenly*) Wait. (*He rises*)

Alice (*turning*) Yes?

Sam I—I'd like to believe you, Alice—but—but—it all sounds a bit strange.

Alice (*smiling sadly*) Perhaps one day, Sam. Perhaps one day.

Sam I'll think about it. Just—just give me time to get things straight in my mind, like.

Alice There's no rush, Sam. I've got all the time in the world.

Sam (*uncertain of what to say*) Aye, I suppose you have.

Alice Give her a kiss from me, will you? Our Terry's girl.

Sam (*nodding*) Aye.

Alice (*turning to the door*) Good-bye, Sam.

Sam (*urgently*) Alice . . .

Alice (*turning*) Yes?

Sam (*taking a deep breath*) I've made me mind up. About what you've just said. (*Quietly*) I believe you.

Alice (*on the verge of tears*) Thank you, Sam. I'm glad.

A small bell tinkles loudly

(*Startled*) Sam . . .

Sam (*spinning round to look behind him*) It were a bell. A little bell.

Alice (*sobbing happily*) It's the signal. They're going to let me in. They're going to accept me.

Sam (*gulping*) I knew they'd see sense in time.

Alice (*flinging her arms around him*) Oh, Sam, love.

Sam (*comforting her*) There, there.

The bell tinkles again

Alice (*dabbing at her eyes*) I'd better go. Mustn't keep them waiting.
Sam (*fighting back tears*) Good luck, Alice. P'raps see you soon, eh?
Alice (*smiling through her tears*) Not for a while yet, Sam. But I'll come for you when it's time.
Sam Promise?
Alice (*nodding*) Promise. (*She leans forward to kiss him*)

The bell tinkles again. Alice straightens and looks upwards

(*Fiercely*) Wait a minute, can't you?

Alice is about to kiss Sam again, when she realizes what she has done. Her face registers consternation, then with resolution she kisses Sam and

Alice hurries out L

Sam gazes after her, as—

the CURTAIN *falls*

FURNITURE AND PROPERTY LIST

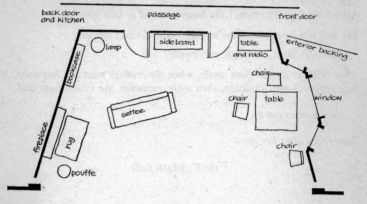

ACT I

SCENE 1

On stage: Settee. *On it:* large cushions of clashing colours, antimacassar
           Pouffe
           3 small chairs
           Square oak table. *On it:* red cloth, cheap vase of imitation flowers
           Sideboard. *On it:* framed wedding photo, ugly vase, old-fashioned
                clock. *In drawers and cupboards:* cloth, cups, saucers, plates, cutlery
                needle and cotton, bottle-opener
           Occasional table. *On it:* old-fashioned radio
           Bookcase with various books, paperbacks, etc.
           Standard lamp
           On walls: period pictures
           On mantelpiece: collection of brass ornaments
           Above mantelpiece: mirror
           In fireplace: fire-irons
           Window curtains (heavy)
           Window curtains (net)
           Carpet
           Scatter rugs

Off stage: Gardening magazine **(Sam)**
           Wicker basket with groceries **(Alice)**
           Fish and chips in newspaper **(Alice)**
           Plate of bread, butter-dish and knife **(Alice)**
           Old electric kettle with worn flex **(Mabel)**
           Cardboard box presumed to contain new kettle **(Sam)**

Personal: **Susan:** purse
                Mabel: cigarette
                Joe: pipe
                Alice: purse with £10 note
                Sam: Two £1 notes

SCENE 2

Strike: Wicker basket
           Gardening magazine
           Everything off table
           Alice's hat and coat
           Cardboard box
           Needle and cotton

Set: Window curtains closed
       Red cloth and flower vase back on table

Off stage: Milk bottles (for **Joe** and **Sam** to rattle)
               2 bottles of beer **(Joe)**
               Large polythene sheet soaked in water **(Joe)**
               2 bath-towels **(Terry)**
               Mug of cocoa **(Sam)**
               Copper warming pan with trick bottom **(Terry)**

Personal: **Susan:** wristwatch, ring

ACT II

SCENE 1

Strike: Beer bottles
           Bath-towel
           Mug of cocoa
           Terry's jacket

Set: Window curtains open
       Wedding photo back on sideboard
       Red cloth and flower vase on sideboard
       White cloth on table
       3 cups, 3 saucers, 4 plates, 4 knives, 3 teaspoons, on table
       Plate of iced buns on table
       Teapot, milk bottle and sugar bowl on table
       Mug of tea by sofa (for **Joe**)
       Tidy room generally

Off stage: Lemon **(Mabel)**
               Fresh tea ready for pot **(Joe)**
               Damp cloth **(Sam)**
               Bowl of trifle **(Joe)**

Scene 2

Strike: Everything off table
             Knife, iced buns, damp cloth, trifle bowl

Set: Red cloth and flower vase back on table
             Small tray on table with teapot, milk jug, sugar bowl, teaspoon
             Mug of tea on sofa (for **Sam**)

Off stage: Tray with 7 cups, saucers, plates, teaspoons, sugar bowl, lemon slices
                  in dish **(Mabel)**
             Teapot, milk jug **(Mabel)**
             Plate of bread and buttered scones **(Terry)**

LIGHTING PLOT

Property fittings required: pendant, wall brackets, standard lamp, coal fire effect
Interior, A living-room. The same scene throughout

ACT I. Scene 1. Morning

To open: General effect of morning light, Fire lit
No cues

ACT I. Scene 2. Evening

To open: Curtains closed. Room in darkness. Fire lit

Cue 1	**Sam** switches on the lights *Snap on practicals*	(Page 23)
Cue 2	**Sam** exits with polythene sheet *Lights flicker and go out, leaving room lit by fire glow*	(Page 31)
Cue 3	**Terry** falls into **Sam**'s arms *Lights flicker then return to opening lighting*	(Page 33)
Cue 4	**Sam** and **Joe** exit *Lights fllcker*	(Page 36)
Cue 5	**Sam** moves to fireplace *Lights flicker and go out—return to cue 2 lighting*	(Page 36)
Cue 6	**Sam:** "Oh, not again." *Lights come on again*	(Page 36)
Cue 7	**Sam:** "Till death do us part." *Lights flicker and go out—return to cue 2 lighting*	(Page 36)
Cue 8	**Sam:** "It seemed that real, too." *Lights flicker and come on again*	(Page 42)

ACT II. Scene 1. Afternoon

To open: General effect of afternoon daylight. Fire lit
No cues

ACT II. Scene 2. Early evening

To open: General effect of early evening daylight. Fire lit

Cue 9	As CURTAIN rises *Slow fade throughout scene to dusk*	(Page 68)

EFFECTS PLOT

ACT I

SCENE 1

No cues

SCENE 2

Cue 1	**Mabel:** "I swear it." *Clap of thunder*	(Page 26)
Cue 2	**Mabel:** ". . . don't you think I won't." *Thunder*	(Page 27)
Cue 3	**Sam:** ". . . that bottle-opener working." *Thunder*	(Page 27)
Cue 4	**Joe** and **Sam** exit *Thunder*	(Page 27)
Cue 5	**Sam** puts hand over **Mabel's** mouth *Thunder*	(Page 28)
Cue 6	**Joe** exits *Thunder*	(Page 29)
Cue 7	**Sam:** "She *couldn't* have been." *Pause, then long rumble of thunder*	(Page 29)
Cue 8	**Sam** exits with polythene sheet *Long rumble of thunder*	(Page 31)
Cue 9	**Sam** and **Joe** exit *Thunder*	(Page 36)
Cue 10	**Sam** moves to fireplace *Thunder*	(Page 36)
Cue 11	**Sam:** "Till death do us part." *Very loud crash of thunder*	(Page 36)

ACT II

SCENE 1

No cues

SCENE 2

No cues